Books by Jan Mitchell

LUCHOW'S GERMAN COOKBOOK

COOKING À LA LONGCHAMPS

COOKING à la LONGCHAMPS

GOOD FOOD—NO NONSENSE

COOKING à la

Illustrations by Betty Church

ESCOFFIER, JR.

Doubleday & Company, Inc.

LONGCHAMPS

Good Food—No Nonsense

By JAN MITCHELL

Preface by CLEVELAND AMORY

Garden City, N.Y. 1964

Library of Congress Catalog Card Number 64-13833
Copyright © 1964 by Janmit Productions Ltd.
All Rights Reserved. Printed in the United States of America
First Edition

To my wife

Preface

BY CLEVELAND AMORY

From time to time—generally ours, unfortunately—restaurateurs and hoteliers are inclined to issue pious pronouncements about a Return to Elegance. It is one thing to issue a pronouncement, however, and another to make it stick. And the sticky fact is that yesterday's "Elegance" was not for everybody. It was an Elegance for the few—propped up by a way of life in which few were called and still fewer chosen.

Today, in contrast, we live in an era which, at its worst, is Elegance for Nobody but, at its best, offers at least the possibility of Elegance for Everybody. And it is a tribute to Jan Mitchell, a restaurateur who came from the Old Way of Life abroad, that he has chosen—in catering to the new era here—what might, in deference to a famous book about his native Sweden, be called the Middle Way.

Brought up in the very lap of a kind of Lapland Aristocracy —he refers, for example, to "our country estates along the Baltic"—and schooled in the *haute cuisine* of the Grand Hotel in Stockholm, he might have been expected to settle down in his New World among the International Settlers at Le Pavillon or The Colony or some other such euphoric emporia. He did not, however. Starting with the purchase of Lüchow's, a great but hardly classifiable caravanserie, he moved on to take over the Restaurants Longchamps—even their affectionate pronunciation, "Long Champs," was, and still is, clear evidence of their basic Americanism.

Once he became owner of this great chain, as well as of the Charles French Restaurant—pride of the Vintage Village Set—Mr. Mitchell set out to pioneer the new and different without, however, breaking with the tried and true. In this book he speaks modestly about restoring tradition—and not the least of the tradition he is restoring is the very word "restore," from *restaurabo*, which, as he tells us in one of his book's most fascinating anecdotes, is the original word from which restaurant was derived. (The entire book, incidentally, is liberally spiced with literary allusions—indicating that unlike so many cookbook authors, not only can Mr. Mitchell write a book but also, on occasion, read one.)

With it all, Mr. Mitchell has not forgotten his meat-and-potatoes customers who want, among other things, their meat and potatoes. Indeed, the very title of this book reveals that he has little patience with the kind of restaurant which gives you all the trimmings—including one to your pocketbook—and little else. And he has even less patience with either food, or, for that matter, wine snobs.

On this latter matter it has long been this writer's thesis that wine snobbery is a mark of the *nouveau riche*. In this book, the wine snob gets his comeuppance, complete with the brickbat statement that there are "many excellent wines" in the United States and the final bouquet prediction that someday this country will have "great wines."

To prove his belief that wine snobbery has held back American wine consumption, Mr. Mitchell, never a man to roll with his lunches without giving proof to his puddings, started a policy of giving, to each customer at dinner, a glass of wine. On all sides he was told that he was committing vintage suicide—that people would stop buying wine at his restaurants. We're not going to tell you how it all turned out, but we are going to say that we believe Mr. Mitchell would have continued his policy in any event. For he is a man who believes, among other things, that every restaurateur is a frustrated party-giver.

There is something, however, which Mr. Mitchell will not share—something for which he is almost as famous as for all the things he does share with others. And it was something noteworthy enough to be a part of his biography in the *Celebrity Register*. "[He] is distinguished," the biography reads sternly, "on the Café Society scene for the fact that he never lets anyone else dance with his wife."

Somehow this too seems part of Jan Mitchell's "Middle Way." A man who has thoroughly embraced the New Way of Life, he still clings, when the fish and chips are down, to the Old Way of Wife.

Recipes for supplementary dishes, sauces, etc., that are printed in small capital letters may be found by consulting the Index.

CONTENTS

Good Food—No Nonsense

JAN MITCHELL
President, Longchamps Restaurants

It was in 1940 that I discovered the Longchamps restaurants and, thereafter, patronized them whenever I was in New York. But it was not until 1950 that I, a bachelor living at the Waldorf Towers, became a Longchamps habitué. At this later time I had, recently, realized a dream of many impatient years. I had purchased Lüchow's, of romantic and gastronomical tradition. And I was occupied, day and night, restoring the charm and cuisine with which August Lüchow, the founder, had endowed this historic restaurant when he had opened its heavy, beamed doors in 1882.

Every now and then, however, I—who love the theater enough to gamble whatever I am able to convince myself I can afford in backing new productions—would play truant. I would leave the Lüchow orchestra playing a Strauss waltz or, perhaps, *The Tales of Hoffmann.* I would leave my patrons tempting themselves with thoughts of German pancakes with kirschwasser for dessert, even as they dined, heartily, on pot roast and potato dumplings with red cabbage, and drank, heartily, of the amber Wurzburger. And I would taxi uptown.

Usually I would have had no dinner. So, when the final curtain fell, my thoughts—no longer absorbed with the dilemma behind the footlights—would turn to visions of a sizzling steak or, had I lunched late and well, a GOLDEN BUCK.

Golden Bucks are among the souvenirs of my youth which

I have, regretfully, put behind me. A restaurateur's life is not a calm one; it exacts some toll.

But a Minute Steak, as it is served at Longchamps, a fine strip streak, thick enough to be grilled to a crusty turn on the outside yet left rare and juicy inside, continues one of my favorite foods. It is also, I frequently observe, a favorite food of those dieters who are dedicated to losing weight painlessly. After thirty years in this country, where there is no need to dress up meat with braising and sauces, I've developed a fondness for the rare beef which horrified me on my first visit here, as it must other visitors from my part of the world.

Or I might, instead of a steak or a Golden Buck, have CRABMEAT A LA DEWEY OR SAUTEED CALVES' LIVER A LA DEUTSCH, two other Longchamps specialties which were then, as they are now, favorites of mine.

After the theater it was to the Longchamps on Broadway at Forty-first Street that I would go. To an excellent captain there I once predicted: "John, you should go far in this business. I've no doubt you'll eventually be manager here!" Not only is John Viale manager there today, he is general manager of all the Longchamps restaurants and I am proud to have him on my staff.

In the morning, usually, it was to the Longchamps on Madison Avenue at Forty-ninth Street, just around two corners from my tower suite, that I would go. Rounding those corners I would consider having the flat, golden-brown omelette that the Longchamps' menu calls OMELETTE PANCAKE STYLE. They do them so well with the freshest eggs. I would consider, too, with more concern for my taste buds than for my waistline, whether I would have my omelette made with cheese or CHICKEN-LIVER MIXTURE.

Invariably, whether I arrived at a Longchamps restaurant for breakfast, dinner, or supper, I would stop to admire the fruit and vegetables in the window. What they would be depended, of course, upon the time of the year; for Longchamps always has been, as it continues to be, a strong advocate of food in the season in which it reaches its finest flavor.

Perhaps a window arrangement would feature green stalks of California asparagus, which is the best asparagus of all. Or Pennsylvania asparagus, which comes next in desirability. The New Jersey "grass" is sandy, the sand seemingly grows in its stalks.

There might be a bright-red tomato—large, even, for a beef-steak—in a small square basket, surrounded with mushrooms the color of ivory. Then I would have regret that mushrooms are so low in food value. But, quickly, this regret would be dispersed by thoughts of the mushroom's subtle taste and its sorcery in invoking the flavor of other foods.

In another basket a lemon-yellow grapefruit might be ruffled with green peas in their pods. Whereupon I would be filled with pity for all the underprivileged breakfast tables prior to 1889 when the grapefruit, thought to be a mutation of a wild fruit and the orange, was first shipped from the island of Jamaica to cities along the eastern seaboard. "The eye-opener fruit" the island growers called it.

The Longchamps displays of fruits and vegetables would remind me of market days in Europe. I would recollect the excitement of the big squares crowded with booths and carts and stands, humming with calls of the farmers, the farm wives, and their children as they arranged and rearranged their produce with such pride that even cabbages became things of beauty. In this country we have no need of such markets. Our supermarkets, with new treats displayed at the turn of every aisle, make every day a market day.

The arrangements in the Longchamps windows had been, I discovered, the fancy of Henry Lustig who, before starting the Longchamps chain in 1920, had owned a fine produce business.

My appetite stimulated by the fresh fruits and vegetables, I would enter the restaurant with anticipation. I was never disappointed. The linen would be immaculate and smooth. The glassware and silver and china would sparkle. The knives would be sharp. The plates would be of a generous size. The lighting would be bright, but not too bright. The chairs would be wide enough to accommodate that portion of the anatomy for which chairs are made. The menu, extensive and varied, would be tempting. And the service was something which I came to applaud as "impersonally personal."

I, who grew up with only women servants in the house, do not care to have men hovering over me. When women hover, I must say, I find it pleasant. At Longchamps I never felt the slightest need for obsequiousness from the dining-room staff. The service itself was fine enough to satisfy my ego. There would be a knowledgeable captain to take my order, a capable waiter to serve it, without unnecessary delay, hot on a hot plate or cold on a cold plate, and a bus boy who would be quick to refill my water glass or replenish the warm crusty rolls and the fresh sweet butter.

In those days I did not dream I would ever own these restaurants. But I should have wondered about this, at least. For the past is the best crystal ball that exists for foreseeing the future. And it had been my history that, very frequently, I would manage to buy that which pleased me.

My pride insists that I could originate should I choose to do so. But, since I find it particularly rewarding to restore restaurants to their former glory, I am partial to establishments that have fond memories for those whose patronage has long been a habit.

Occasionally I wonder what would have become of me had I been born a century and a half earlier, before restaurants came into being. A man named Boulanger, proprietor of a soup kitchen in Paris, was the originator of restaurants. In 1765 he added two or three items to his menu and posted a sign which read: VENITE OMNES, QUI STOMACHO LABORATIS ET EGO RESTAURABO VOS, meaning, in English, "Come, all ye who labor on your stomach and I shall restore you." From *restaurabo*, for restore, came the word restaurants.

Not for another twenty-five years, however, did restaurants come into their own. Then the great chefs, unable, after the

French Revolution, to find employment in the châteaux and palaces, deigned to bestow their culinary genius upon restaurant kitchens. And their prized dishes, with which they had pleased royalty and the nobility, became the specialties of the house.

Only this is certain, one way or another my absorbing interest in food would have prevailed.

As a small boy I used to bribe the family servants with little gifts, bought with my savings, for permission to assist at the big stoves and ovens. And when we would leave our home in the city for our country estate along the Baltic, I was always in a state of high excitement at the prospect of the big hunting parties for which all manner of food, dramatically presented, was prepared.

I can remember, too, as if it were yesterday instead of forty-odd years ago, the sight and taste of the white, pink, and chocolate MERINGUES we used to find in our Christmas stockings. I besieged our cook to teach me how to beat egg whites and sugar into these puffs. I went to my father's library and read, in the "M" volume of the encyclopedia, how these *pâtisseries* had originated early in the eighteenth century. And I was delighted to discover, in a notation less appetite-depressing than encyclopedic references to food are likely to be, that Queen Marie Antoinette had loved these sweetmeats so well she had gone to the palace kitchens to concoct them.

My dream of owning Lüchow's, after I had dined there in 1932, on my first visit to America, changed the entire pattern of my life. Upon my return to Sweden, I told my family I had no wish to settle down as a country squire and eventually fall in love with a young lady of the local gentry. Instead, I said, I wished to learn the restaurant business and make my home in the United States where I had already fallen in love with a restaurant.

Fortunately, my parents could comprehend how individuality can be stronger than tradition. They allowed me, after completing my studies at the universities of Prague and Zurich, to enter a school of hotel management in Switzerland. Following this, I served an apprenticeship in the kitchens and dining rooms of many European hotels, among others the renowned Grand Hotel of Stockholm.

When, in 1940, I returned to the United States, Lüchow's was not for sale. Nor was there any immediate prospect that it would be for sale. I could only wait for the retirement of Victor Eckstein, proprietor since the death of his uncle-in-law, August Lüchow. I could only let it be known that I was interested and that it was my intention to preserve the atmosphere, traditions, and cuisine that had caused Lüchow's to be described as "more than a restaurant, a way of life."

Those who have been driven by a compulsion will understand my long and unremitting obsession with this restaurant. Those who have not could not.

Providentially, together with my propensity for "seeing big," I inherited a healthy degree of business acumen. I knew, therefore, that if I was to offer my patrons the best values I must, in all departments, manage my establishments wisely. To this end I enrolled in a summer course in business management for which, frequently, I have reason to be grateful.

I lived, first, in Washington where I initiated my practice of buying what pleased me when I became the owner of an old restaurant which I had regularly patronized. At once, I set about to reclaim its earlier reputation.

For eight years, while this restaurant flourished gratifyingly, I made frequent trips to New York and, needless to say, to Lüchow's. Then, at last, in 1950, Lüchow's was mine.

It was soon after this that I began making my way to whichever Longchamps restaurant was most convenient. Nine years later, in control of 86 per cent of the Longchamps stock, I became president of this luxury chain.

I bought the Longchamps restaurants because I liked them. But my business sense also influenced this transaction in which I invested several million dollars. The restaurants had gone downhill under the absentee management which had prevailed after the federal government had sold Longchamps because of Henry Lustig's tax problems. But I found it preposterous that any business which grossed eight million dollars a year, as this chain did, should lose money. I was certain I could turn the losses into gains. As I have.

I also wanted—I might even say coveted—the great purchasing power this acquisition has given me. Where the average restaurateur buys fifty ribs I buy 500. When I stand at my warehouse door, flanked by my executive chef, Ernest Imhof, and our staff, to check in deliveries it is more a matter of habit than necessity. I know the ribs and loins that come off the meat trucks will be those I selected so critically at the packing houses. I have no doubt I will receive exactly those crates of fruits and vegetables on which I bid as they came off the boat or truck. I am convinced the barrels of fish will be those I chose, at dawn, at Fulton Market. I have every reason to expect that all the things I ordered and stamped with my stamp will arrive in perfect order. No purveyor would, knowingly, risk the loss of my business; not only because of its volume but because, if I may be immodest enough to say so, it is a mark of distinction to supply Lüchow's, Longchamps, and my latest purchase, Charles French Restaurant on the Avenue of the Americas.

The first changes I made at Longchamps were behind the scenes. I ordered new refrigerators and ranges. I put in air conditioning where it did not exist. I replaced small equipment down to the smallest details of spatulas and wooden spoons, carving knives and forks, sieves and colanders.

Women, I notice, will work, happily enough, in inadequately equipped kitchens. If there is no omelette pan they will make an iron frying pan do. This I do not applaud. I believe all workers are entitled to proper tools. But I do make a deep bow to women for their adaptability. Men do not have it, as was illustrated by the immediate rise in the spirit and morale of the chefs, cooks, and kitchen boys when I restored the Longchamps kitchens to a high point of efficiency.

Next, I had the great good fortune to engage, as executive chef for the Longchamps chain, Ernest Imhof, formerly executive chef of the Savoy-Plaza. This meant that, relieved of the need for constant supervision backstage, I could begin making changes out front.

Always the Longchamps restaurants have had the same décor: Chinese red and gold. It was handsome enough. But I felt each restaurant should reflect its milieu. Therefore, dipping into my reassuring profits, I began redecorating my restaurants.

The restaurant at City Hall now reflects the old Dutch influence which used to prevail on the lower end of Manhattan Island. Uptown on the newly fashionable Third Avenue, in the very fashionable Manhattan House, the décor is reminiscent of the pleasure pavilions of eighteenth- and nineteenth-century Europe. However, the lower glass-walled dining room still looks out on the wide terrace, landscaped and furnished with umbrella tables.

Oliver Smith, the scenic designer responsible for the beautiful settings of *My Fair Lady* and *Camelot*, has also executed architectural and decorative changes at other Longchamps.

The restaurant in the Empire State Building has been transformed into a replica of a Mississippi river boat, colorful and romantic enough to fill Mark Twain himself with nostalgia for the gay old days.

The Longchamps at Lexington Avenue and Forty-second Street, just a stone's throw from Grand Central Station, is, appropriately, comfortably reminiscent of an old *à la carte* Pullman car.

And the elegant new décor of our restaurant at Twelfth Street on Fifth Avenue, with its famous outdoor cafe, was inspired by an English inn of the Regency period with an Ascot Bar.

Other things, also, have been accomplished.

Ever mindful of the produce business from which Longchamps came to be I continue to have fruit and vegetable displays in the windows. And I hope it again will be my pleasure, as it was when I first took over these restaurants, to offer—compliments of the house—portions of the delicacy of the month.

For some time now at dinner a glass of white or red wine, Chablis or Reisling, rosé or Burgundy, has been served with the compliments of the house. And the menu suggests a wine to complement each entree.

When I decided to serve patrons a complimentary glass of wine I was warned:

"You will ruin your wine sales!"

Nevertheless, eager to play some small part in furthering the growing appreciation of wine in this country, I persisted. (Please see the chapter entitled "Good Wine—No Nonsense.")

The warnings about diminishing sales have not been borne out. Fewer glasses of wine are sold, yes; but there has been a marked increase in the sales of bottles and half bottles. The glass of wine that goes to every place with my compliments seems to intrigue the appetite.

The hours between five and seven at Longchamps I would not miss. As I watch my patrons arrive I, like the frustrated party-giver that I believe all restaurateurs to be, cannot wait for them to taste the dishes in preparation in the ovens and on the stoves . . . ROAST LEG OF LAMB LONGCHAMPS with little new potatoes, with parsley flakes and butter; in season, of course . . . CURRIED FRESH SEAFOOD CALCUTTA, with lobster, shrimp, crabmeat, and scallops served with fluffy, long-grained rice and chutney covered with a delectably rich, yellow sauce. Jealously, I watch my regular patrons as they come in or await friends, to see if they wear the quietly pleased look of those who anticipate a good dinner.

Between the hours of five and seven there's the sound of

ice being shaken at the bar. Flames burn under chafing dishes. Little SPICY COCKTAIL MEATBALLS heat in one, plump cocktail sausages in the other. I beam at the guests waiting at the complimentary buffet table for the carving steward, with his high white hat, to carve the ham, the turkey or the corned brisket of beef and lay it on the miniature slices of crusty French bread. And, inevitably, I find myself admiring not only the steward's deftness in carving but his appreciation for the thickness at which a meat or bird will be tastiest.

There is, of course, nothing new about a carving steward! The early Roman gourmand, Lucullus, is reported to have paid his steward a sum equal to several thousands annually; a fortune in those days.

It is with regret that I finally quit the Longchamps cocktail hour, my conscience prodding me toward my latest acquisition, Charles, which still needs careful supervision. As I head for the door I see Ernest Imhof shaking his distinguished head at a young woman who protests her escort's making another trip to the buffet table, telling her, warmly, paternally, "But at Longchamps we are unhappy if people do not enjoy to eat!"

The lengthy and spirited menu conferences that Chef Imhof and I have corroborate this. Our conferences often remind me of Prince Talleyrand, whose scruples were as underdeveloped as the palate was overdeveloped. He used to confer with his chef for exactly one hour every morning about the dishes that were to be served at dinner that evening.

Some of us, unquestionably, come into the world with a stronger sense of taste and smell than others. No longer, I notice, does my wife of several years—the former English actress, Ellin Hobbins—smile, in her enchantingly indulgent way, when I insist that I can tell if a roast beef is going to be juicy and sweet by the way it smells when it is cooking.

Every day, too, Ernest Imhof and I hold tasting sessions. Small portions of many foods are set before us. At these sessions I give thanks for my acute taste buds, also my total recall of flavor which enables me to remember exactly how a dish, ideally, should taste.

Invariably, as Ernest Imhof and I smack our lips, in the approved taster's fashion, we say together, "How about some more sherry" or "Needs a little more pepper."

To work with him is my never-ending pleasure. His respect for the kitchen and those who have, over the years, contributed to it is great; is, in fact, his theme for the next chapter, which, typically, he's chosen to call "No Dish Can Be Any Better Than Its Ingredients."

Both Chef Imhof and I are partial to food with a true flavor. For in this rich land, where the best of most food is available, there is no need for any such culinary didos as abound in the history of cuisine.

Frederick the Great, for instance, is said to have insisted upon making his own coffee, using champagne instead of water, adding a bit of powdered mustard for a little kick-back in flavor.

Alexandre Dumas, in his *Dictionary of Cuisine*, tells how Louis XVIII had a jury test fruit before it was served him, had his chops broiled between other chops, and his truffled ortolans—small birds somewhat resembling the American bobolink—roasted within the stomachs of partridges.

Always, however, I am reluctant to disapprove of any culinary experiments, however recherché they may be. For, over the years, those who have had and have catered to an overwhelming interest in food have enriched our table. It is the prejudices and the inhibitions about food that should be deplored. They limit the opportunity the American kitchen has, right now, to go forward. For American men, who undoubtedly held back our national cookery by their insistence upon familiar dishes—steak and fried chicken and roast beef, preferably—have returned from military and commercial sojourns in every part of the world with less provincial tastes than they had when they went away. Therefore, the American woman, *circa* 1964, is blessed with such an opportunity to improve her table as never existed before.

For anyone to be prejudiced or intimidated by foreign dish names is a pity. Dish names, naturally, reflect the countries in which dishes originated, often years before the American colonies were settled.

Explore the dishes with the fanciest names and, again and again, you will discover they first appeared in regional cooking because their ingredients were easily and profusely available in that part of the country and, gradually, because they were good food, came to have wider and wider popularity. Just like our southern CORN FRITTERS and CANDIED SWEET POTATOES, our Vermont ROASTED TURKEYS and our CLAM CHOWDERS.

Take, for instance, a few of the international items to be found on a Longchamps menu: beef Chateaubriand, petits fours, curries, BOUILLABAISSE.

The QUICHE LORRAINE, which currently enjoys great popularity, was the frugal farm wives' way of using the cheese they had made to save excess milk. The quiche, or kiche as it's sometimes spelled, undoubtedly originated in Germany.

A Chateaubriand is nothing more—and there are those who would insist there *is* nothing more—than thick slices of the choice center cut of a beef filet, grilled and served with or without SAUCE BEARNAISE or Sauce Colbert, as it used to be prepared to delight the gourmet novelist whose name it bears.

It was the great pastry chef, Carême, who reigned over the kitchens of French palaces, who gave the name of petits fours to the little cakes that crowd a Longchamps dessert tray. He called these cakes, made of a size that would bake quickly in the dying fires, after the day's important baking was over, petits fours; in other words, little fires.

One day at luncheon time I overheard a young wife complimenting one of our captains on the emince of curried chicken. "My husband," she said, "acquired a taste for curry during his service in the Far East. But I'm timid about attempting to make any curried dish. . . ."

I stepped forward and bowed. "Madame," I said, "if you use herbs and spices you, in effect, use curry. Curry is a combination of about fifteen herbs and spices which have been dried and powdered. How hot curry is depends upon the amount of chili powder that has gone into the mixture. Do not be intimidated by curry! Use just a little. Taste. Add a little more."

She smiled. "You give me courage. I have left-over lamb that should be delicious, curried, with chutney. My husband will be so surprised!"

BOUILLABAISSE, to which Thackeray was moved to write a ballad, is, literally, a soup stew made with a variety of seafood but always, the traditionalists insist, with the spiny lobster and saffron. Understandably, bouillabaisse is native to the Mediterranean coast where fish is abundant. And at Marseilles, where bouillabaisse is justifiably famous, they bake a special bread, *marette*, to go with it, of a texture excellent for dunking or wiping a platter clean of the last smudge of saffron-flavored broth.

In ancient days bouillabaisse was believed to be a soporific. An amusing legend has it that Venus, the goddess of love, used to prepare this soup stew for Vulcan, her consort, when she wanted him to sleep soundly and long so she might go about her affairs.

When Doubleday & Company, publishers of my Lüchow's cookbook, approached me with the idea of a Longchamps cookbook I was pleased. But I also was puzzled as to what this book should be called. To name my Lüchow book, filled with German-Viennese recipes, was a simple matter; *Lüchow's German Cookbook*. But the Longchamps menu of over one hundred items is international.

"The title," I told myself, as I lay awake one night, "should exemplify the Longchamps cuisine." When I awoke the next morning I had the title, which must have been in the back of my mind, waiting: *Cooking à la Longchamps* with the subtitle *Good Food—No Nonsense.*

Cookbooks crowd the shelves of the booksellers. There are those which concentrate upon the recipes of different countries. There are others which offer recipes for one particular food. There are innumerable so-called gourmet cookbooks. There is, also, Alexandre Dumas' *Dictionary of Cuisine*, from which I have quoted and which I recommend for every bedside table. There are essays on food. There are histories of food. And there is Prosper Montagne's *Larousse Gastronomique*, a fascinating encyclopedia of cuisine of over one million words.

But in no bookstore have I been able to find a book dedicated, as this is, to:

Good Food—No Nonsense

Which is very odd. For about good food there is no nonsense.

No Dish Can Be Any Better Than Its Ingredients

ERNEST IMHOF

Executive Chef, Longchamps Restaurants; Treasurer, Executive Chefs de Cuisine Association; Member of Helvetia Culinary Society; Member of La Société des Amis d'Escoffier

In recent years I have, on many occasions, pondered on the rapidity with which our lives can change. My life changed, most fortuitously, in exactly ten minutes. And on the basis of nothing more complicated than an old-fashioned handshake.

On a spring morning in 1959 I met with Jan Mitchell, President of Longchamps, in his office. Without preamble, for he is a most direct man, he said to me: "Mr. Imhof, it is my ambition to make the Longchamps cuisine a byword in New York. To this end I would like you to be Longchamps' Executive Chef."

I was, at the time, Executive Chef of the Savoy Hilton. However, aware of Mr. Mitchell's reputation in the restaurant world and challenged by his plans for his restaurants, I answered, at once: "To be associated with you will be my pleasure!"

Whereupon we shook hands. There is no better contract. Legal phrases will not stand in the way of anyone who means to be dishonest.

In my entire career I have never been happier nor had greater enthusiasm for my work than I have now. When I first came to Longchamps I knew excitement in the challenge of re-establishing the kitchens so they not only would equal but excel their former excellence. Now I have the challenge of keeping our menu of over one hundred items temptingly diversified, so it will appeal to all tastes and, at all times, take full advantage of the foods that are at their best because they are in season.

It is a never ending source of satisfaction to me to watch the old Longchamps clientele return to our dining rooms. And I am constantly gratified, as I know Mr. Mitchell to be, by our large patronage from the musical, operatic, theatrical, art, journalistic, and literary worlds.

Years ago the hotels and restaurants that had a fine cuisine were supported by society. No longer is this true. Today it is men and women from business and the professions who are the gourmets and whose patronage, therefore, both restaurateurs and executive chefs mark with justifiable pride.

The celebrated Longchamps' habitués are too numerous to mention. At our restaurant across from the Metropolitan Opera House we serve, among many others, Elisabeth Schwarzkopf, Rudolf Firkusny, Cesare Siepi, Dorothy Kirsten, Dame Alicia Markova, and John Brownlee, Director of the Manhattan School of Music. We also frequently serve Joan Sutherland and Licia Albanese for whom I have prepared dishes, included in this book, which bear their names. And frequent supper patrons are pianist Byron Janis and conductors Antal Dorati and Henri René. Kitty Carlisle, Bud Collyer, Betsy Palmer, Mary Martin, and Lillian and Dorothy Gish lunch and dine at our Sixty-fifth Street restaurant. So does Rudy Vallee, one of our many patrons partial to BREAST OF CHICKEN SAUTE EUGENIE. Tom Poston, Arlene Francis, Barry Nelson, Dina Merrill, Beatrice Lillie, Alfred Drake, and General Lucius Clay are to be glimpsed at our tables. So are

Hallie Burnett, the novelist, and her husband, Whit Burnett, editor and publisher. The Burnetts are most likely to order FILET OF SOLE CAPRICE or CHICKEN SAUTE WITH RED WINE. Hildegarde, the *chanteuse*, who dines at Forty-ninth Street and Madison Avenue, not far from her midtown apartment, never seems to tire of our CHICKEN CHOW MEIN. And I am always pleased to see Paul Newman and Joanne Woodward, Barbra ("Funny Girl") Streisand, Mike Nichols, and Carol Channing at our Mark Twain River Boat restaurant in the Empire State Building. Or to find Elizabeth Taylor and Richard Burton having an after-theater snack there.

Frequently, Longchamps patrons ask me how I decided to become a chef. It is a question I find it impossible to answer. I never remember thinking about this. I just knew, as I grew up in Switzerland, even before I was sixteen years old, that I would be a chef. As far back as memory goes I can see myself at my mother's heels whenever she was in the kitchen of our home in Switzerland. My enjoyment at licking the pots and pans was great, but quite secondary to my sense of excitement as I watched food being prepared and wrinkled my young nose, in delight, at the aromas that came from the stove and the oven.

My first attempt at cooking was an omelette, pancake style. It turned out not too badly. But over the slow fire of our wood-burning stove it did not go fast enough to please me. I had not yet learned the importance of patience in good cookery.

It seems to be the history of chefs that they early know what they want to do. Carême, a chef of kings, when he was cast out as a young lad by his desperate father who had twenty-five children to feed, chose to knock on the door of a pastry shop and ask for work.

Louis Diat, noted chef at the Ritz Hotels in Paris and London before he came to the United States to establish and supervise the *haute cuisine* of the New York Ritz-Carlton,

knew when he was fifteen that the kitchen was his métier.
And when the great Escoffier embarked upon his life's
work he was barely twelve.

It was my privilege to meet Escoffier when, during his visit
to the Zurich Culinary Exhibition in the 1930s, he stopped
at the Hotel Baur au Lac where I was a young cook. He was
an old man then, in his eighties. His hair and his big mus-
tache were snow white. But he carried himself with purpose
and confidence. And he wore his decorations; the cross of a
chevalier of the Legion of Honor and the rosette of an officer
of the legion—conferred upon him because of the prestige he
had brought to the art of French cooking—with both dignity
and pride.

It was of Escoffier, as it always is of Escoffier, that my
confreres of *La Société des Amis d'Escoffier* and I talked
last winter over the *pâté* in crust and the pheasants in paprika
and cream, with sauerkraut—no other vegetable would do—
that I served when it was my turn to entertain. Like those
who had been hosts before me, I sought, if possible, to excel
those dinners which had preceded mine.

There have been chefs more famous than Escoffier but
only because they exercised greater showmanship. Carême, for
instance, would not be so famous had he not had the wealth
of kings to squander. He used to spend weeks designing his
architectural *pâtisseries* and weeks more, with countless as-
sistants, working on their construction.

It is Escoffier for whom I, and most chefs, have the high-
est esteem. Even as he made the kitchens of both London's
Savoy Hotel and Carlton Hotel world famous he had to consider costs. The way most chefs do. Hotels and restaurants
are run for profit not for loss. This I consider a quite proper
state of affairs. Dishes created mainly for their pretension
contribute little, I am convinced, to the classic principles of
haute cuisine.

There has never been a time, since I served my apprenticeship at the Lausanne Palace in Switzerland, that I have not had to be mindful of the money that was going out against the money that was coming in.

At the Hotel Kulm in Saint-Moritz, where for eight years I was the youngest of executive chefs and created many dishes for the pleasure of royalty, diplomats, and film stars, an entry in red ink would have been frowned upon.

The same judgment applied at the Grand Hotel in Stockholm. There, many times, I had the honor of shaking hands with Gustav, King of Sweden, a true gourmet. Also at the Park Lane Hotel in London, where Winston Churchill, the Prince of Wales—now H.R.H. the Duke of Windsor—and H.R.H. the late Duke of Kent were frequent guests. And at the Hotel Baur-au-Lac in Zurich where King Boris of Bulgaria was among the renowned guests.

And it was not otherwise when, in the 1930s, I was assistant chef at the Swiss Pavilion at the World's Fair or during my fifteen years as executive chef of the Savoy Plaza which, when Conrad Hilton bought it, became the Savoy Hilton.

However, it has been my good fortune that the *hôteliers* and restaurateurs with whom I have been associated have, in addition to their executive abilities, had an appreciation of fine food.

In my relationship with Jan Mitchell, president of the Longchamps chain, I am especially fortunate. He, an excellent executive and organizer, is also a connoisseur of food and wine, with his heart in the kitchen.

At Longchamps we subscribe to the basic principle of cuisine that no dish can be any better than what goes into it. We often go far afield for our food supplies. Our red snapper and pompano and abalone are flown from Florida, our sturgeon and salmon from Nova Scotia. Our sole comes by air from the English Channel. Our chickens, which arrive by special truck, are plump and tender, never having run on the ground, having always been kept on wire mesh. Our sardines are shipped from the Mediterranean. Our brislings come from Norway.

There are many phases of my many activities at Longchamps which I enjoy, but none more than my fortnightly meetings with our chefs. Among other business we will usually discuss a new dish that is being added to the menu. As one chef prepares this dish and the others watch, I explain why it must be done just this way and, importantly, how it must be served.

Following these meetings each chef returns to the kitchen over which he presides, to pass on what has been said and done to his staff of about twenty people.

At Longchamps we specialize in beef items which are the most popular, especially our HAMBURGER STEAK of chopped sirloin, served with buttered fresh leaf spinach and mashed potatoes and our LONDON BROIL, which, sliced on a long diagonal, is succulent and tender, served with fresh broccoli spears polonnaise and Long Branch potatoes.

Among our most enjoyed fish dishes are BROOK TROUT SAUTE AMANDINE and FILET OF SOLE CAPRICE, with glazed bananas and almonds.

When a party buffet is set up in one of our private dining rooms, I, a seasoned chef of many years, find myself as eager as any young man who has just earned his *toque blanche*. It is my pleasure, irrespective of how busy I may be, to supervise the arrangement of the table and the preparation of any special dish.

In 1958, I had the honor to be awarded the first prize for Practical and Artistic Buffets by the Société Culinaire Philanthropique. This sent my thoughts back to the Palace Hotel at Locarno where I was chef during the conferences that produced the pact. Those attending these conferences were of many races and faiths; among others, Sir Austen Chamberlain, Mussolini, and Gustav Stresemann of Germany. Not only were there foods which these eminent gentlemen preferred—since the appetite tends to grow on what it feeds on—

there were also foods which were demanded by medical and religious diets.

I solved the problem of the many varied items required daily, by a long buffet that offered the native dishes of all the countries represented; this, of course, in addition to the hotel's regular menu. However, the buffet, at which many gentlemen developed a fondness for the dishes of other countries, proved so popular that orders from the menu were few.

The very appearance of a fine buffet is, in itself, appetizing. At Longchamps when there is a party in a private dining room I find myself walking around the tiered table, admiring the ice sculpture of a swan with the gray-black eggs of beluga caviar nested between its wings. Solicitously, I take another sprig of parsley from my *garde-manger*, who accompanies me on my inspection, and tuck it beneath the poached salmon in aspic. I have the long platter for the asparagus stalks placed beside the salver on which a bed of water cress awaits the individually roasted chickens, which will be bordered with fluted mushrooms, braised onions, and golden potato straws. I rehearse, again, with my *garde-manger* how, at the proper time, this table will be wheeled out to make way for the dessert buffet with its baskets of fruit, trays of cheese, shallow cups of strawberries and raspberries with a kiss of kirsch, coffee service, and other sweets.

On a classic buffet there are no flowers. It is presumed the food will be prepared and displayed in a manner that will sufficiently adorn the table.

There also are other rules for the buffet:

It should offer hot and cold food.

Dishes should have a contrast in texture as well as in color.

Every item should be presented so it pleases the eye and tempts the palate.

There should be something new and provocative, to provide an element of surprise.

The preference and diets of the guests should receive consideration.

A home menu might be:

EMINCE OF CHICKEN MEXICAINE

RICE PILAF

Cold Roast Beef

SEAFOOD A LA NEWBURG in *Chafing Dish*

Crusty Hot Bread

Butter

MACEDOINE OF FRUIT *with Kirsch*
> Served with thin slices of poundcake or petits fours

Cheese Tray

Coffee

Or, instead of the Emince of Chicken Mexicaine, Rice Pilaf, Cold Roast Beef, and Seafood à la Newburg, a buffet might offer:

FILET OF BEEF STROGANOFF in *Chafing Dish*

EGG NOODLES

COLD POACHED SALMON
> Garnished with halves of hard-boiled eggs, small tomatoes or tomato quarters, and MAYONNAISE or GREEN MAYONNAISE with finely minced herbs.

Together, Mr. Mitchell and I have chosen the recipes that appear in this book. Many of them are those which are most frequently requested by our patrons. None of them require ingredients which are not generally available.

I wish that, in closing, I could say that on Sundays it is my custom to prepare special dishes for my family. But that would not be true. I test-taste so many dishes during the week that on Sundays I am hungry only for the simplest fare. At our dinner table my wife and sons are apt to tease me:

"Shoemakers' children go unshod. Executive chefs' children eat boiled beef, potatoes, and vegetables!"

I make no apology for boiled beef, potatoes, and vegetables. Very good this simple dish can be; another example of this book's title: cooking à la Longchamps, *good food—no nonsense.*

Canapés, Hors d'Oeuvres, and Appetizers

"What is the difference between a canapé and an hors d'oeuvre?"

That is an often-asked question.

Canapés are strips, rounds, triangles, or squares of thin toast, often sautéed—or substitute crackers or biscuits—that are spread with appetizing mixtures, either hot or cold.

Hors d'oeuvres are meat, fish, poultry, cheese, eggs, or vegetables—prepared with sauce, spices, herbs, or dressing—which are eaten in the hand or from a toothpick or from a plate.

Canapés and hors d'oeuvres—and hors d'oeuvres may include canapés—are believed to have been introduced into cuisine by the frugal housewives of France, Scandinavia, Italy, and Russia, where they are known, respectively, as hors d'oeuvres, smorgasbord, antipasto, and *zakuski*. The European housewife, instinctively economical whether she lives in a big city house or a small farm cottage, discovered that canapés and hors d'oeuvres, by any name, are an appetizing way of combining leftovers either as a first course at table or as an accompaniment to predinner wine.

Those with culinary pride see to it that canapés and hors d'oeuvres offer a contrast to the food that is to follow, season them so they stimulate the appetite, and present them so they are a joy to the eye and thus inviting to the palate. After many years as a restaurateur I continue to marvel at the fillip food receives from such touches as a piping of anchovy butter or a bit of grated hard-boiled egg—yolk or white.

At Longchamps an increasingly popular luncheon is a plate of assorted hors d'oeuvres, coffee, and dessert. Our hors d'oeuvres, of course, vary. Some appear and disappear as their ingredients come in and go out of season. But there is such variety that the temporary absence of one or two is unimportant. . . .

Celery stuffed with Roquefort; CHICKEN-LIVER PATE; marinated artichoke hearts; smoked clams, mussels, or trout; green and black olives; radish roses; little pastry boats or tartlets of SEAFOOD or LOBSTER A LA NEWBURG or CHICKEN A LA KING; mushrooms in wine; tomato and cucumber slices with a touch of thyme and a sprig of dill; herrings and onion rings in sour cream; the elegant Italian ham, prosciutto, sliced as thin as the Genoese salami or the hotly spiced sausage; DEVILED STUFFED EGGS, celery root, caviar, pickled beets, and shrimps.

Many hors d'oeuvres require little or no preparation. Others, expecially tempting, do. Directions for many of these as well as those which appear above in small capital letters will be found on the next several pages.

Once, on a holiday in New Orleans, I bought the entire catch of a shrimp boat; big shrimp that would, I knew, have a tempting nutty flavor when they were boiled just long enough to turn pink all over. Restaurateurs, like all good hosts and hostesses, are constantly on the lookout for a food find and, coming upon one, will, excitedly, plan an entirely new menu around it.

CHICKEN TIDBITS

(Hors d'oeuvre for 6 to 8)

3 tablespoons butter	½ teaspoon salt
1½ tablespoons flour	¼ teaspoon pepper
1 cup milk	1 tablespoon finely chopped
2 cups cooked, finely	chives, fresh or frozen
chopped chicken	Flour
¼ cup cooked, chopped	1 egg, beaten
mushrooms	Fresh bread crumbs
¼ cup sherry	Fat for deep-fat frying
5 egg yolks	
1 teaspoon arrowroot or	
cornstarch	

Melt butter in a saucepan, stir in flour smoothly and cook several minutes without browning. Pour in milk and cook over a low heat, stirring constantly, for 10 minutes. Now stir in chicken, mushrooms, sherry, and continue cooking for 5 to 10 minutes longer. Combine egg yolks with arrowroot or cornstarch and add to chicken. Cook, stirring constantly, until mixture bubbles. Remove from heat and season with salt, pepper, chives. Pour into an oiled flat dish and cool.

Shape into balls the size of a walnut, coat with flour, dip into well-beaten egg, and cover with bread crumbs. Fry a few at a time in deep fat, heated to 375° F on a thermometer (or until a 1-inch cube of bread browns in 40 seconds). Drain. Serve with a hot curry sauce or any other suitable sauce.

SPICY COCKTAIL MEATBALLS

(Yield: 30 to 40 meatballs)

½ *pound ground beef*
½ *pound ground pork*
½ *pound ground veal*
½ *cup fresh white bread crumbs*
¼ *cup light cream*
2 *tablespoons of chopped parsley*
2 *tablespoons of chopped onions, cooked until tender*

1 *tablespoon of curry powder*
2 *tablespoons of chopped chutney*
3 *whole eggs*
Salt to taste
2 *tablespoons of butter*

Mix above thoroughly, with the exception of the butter, and shape into balls about 1 inch in diameter. Heat the butter in a skillet large enough to accommodate the meatballs easily. Brown balls evenly all around over a medium heat for about 10 minutes. Shake the pan occasionally. Remove skillet from the heat and transfer the balls to a platter.

CURRY SAUCE

2 *tablespoons of butter*	1 *teaspoon of curry powder*
1 *tablespoon of flour*	*Juice of 1 lemon*
¼ *cup of sherry*	*Salt to taste*
1 *cup hot light cream*	

Place butter in a skillet and blend in the flour with a wire whisk. Pour in the sherry and cream, stirring occasionally. Return to the heat, bring to boil and let cook 5 minutes, stirring occasionally. Add curry powder, lemon juice, and salt to taste. Return meatballs to the sauce and let simmer over low heat for 15 to 20 minutes. Transfer to a serving dish or chafing dish. Spike each meatball with a tooth or frilled pick. Serve hot!

HOMEMADE LIVER PATE

(Makes 6 to 8 servings)

2 *medium onions, sliced thin*	½ *teaspoon salt*
¼ *cup chicken fat or butter*	*Pinch of pepper*
¼ *cup chicken broth* (See note below)	2 *cloves*
⅓ *pound fat back, cut in strips*	1 *bay leaf*
1 *pound chicken livers*	¼ *teaspoon dried thyme*
½ *pound pork liver, cut into chunks*	½ *cup water*
	2 *eggs, beaten*
	½ *cup heavy cream*
	½ *cup sherry*
	1 *tablespoon cornstarch*

Cook onions in heated chicken fat or butter, and chicken broth until tender. Sauté fat back for several minutes in a skillet, then add both kinds of liver, onions, and the fat in which they cooked, salt, pepper, cloves, bay leaf, thyme, and water. Cook to a boil, cover and continue cooking over a low heat for about 30 minutes or until liver is tender.

Drain and grind in a food grinder or blend in an electric blender until mixture is fine. Stir in eggs, cream, and almost all of the sherry. Combine cornstarch with remaining sherry to make a smooth paste and mix into the pâté. Cook, stirring constantly, until bubbly. Remove from heat; taste and adjust seasoning if necessary. Pack into a crock or mold. Cover and refrigerate. If pâté isn't to be eaten immediately, melt a little butter and pour it over the top to seal before covering and refrigerating. Serve with toast strips or rounds.

Note: 1 chicken bouillon cube dissolved in ¼ cup boiling water will provide the broth.

SWISS CHEESE CROQUETTES [*Délices de Gruyère*]
(Serves 4 to 6)

Croquettes:

3 *tablespoons butter*
4 *tablespoons flour*
1½ *cups milk*
1 *teaspoon salt*
Dash white pepper
Dash nutmeg

4 *egg yolks*
½ *pound* (2½ *cups*)
    grated Swiss cheese
Fat for deep-fat frying
TOMATO SAUCE

Breading:

2 *tablespoons flour*
1 *egg, well beaten*
1 *cup fine dry bread crumbs*

Melt butter in a saucepan. Stir in flour smoothly and cook a minute or two. Pour in milk and cook over a moderate heat, stirring constantly until very thick and bubbly. Continue cooking over a low heat for about 5 minutes. Stir in salt, pepper, nutmeg, egg yolks, and grated cheese. Beat thoroughly while mixture bubbles for about a second. Remove from heat, pour on a flat platter, and refrigerate for 2 to 3 hours.

Mold into balls the size of large walnuts. Coat with flour, dip into well-beaten egg, then roll in crumbs. Fry in deep fat heated to 375° F on fat thermometer (or until a 1-inch cube of bread browns in 40 seconds) for 3 to 4 minutes. Croquettes should be crusty brown on the outside. Drain on paper towels.

Serve hot with Tomato Sauce for lunch or as an hors d'oeuvre.

CHEESE BUTTER DIPS

1 *pound imported Swiss cheese, grated*	½ *cup water*
½ *cup heavy cream*	*Salt, pepper, and nutmeg to taste*
1 *pound soft sweet butter*	

Mix cheese and cream thoroughly and force through fairly coarse sieve. Beat butter with water until fluffy. Add cheese mixture to beaten butter and blend thoroughly. Season with salt, pepper, and nutmeg.

Variations

This cheese-butter base may be used with many variations. For example:

20 parts of cheese butter to 1 part purée of anchovies

8 parts of cheese butter to 1 part French mustard

10 parts of cheese butter to 7 parts diced bologna and 2 parts French mustard

4 parts of cheese butter to 1 part finely chopped egg yolk

4 parts of cheese butter to 1 part diced red pepper

10 parts of cheese butter to 7 parts finely chopped ham, 3 parts diced dill pickle, and 2 parts French mustard

8 *parts of cheese butter to 2 parts of diced pineapple and 1 part of French mustard*

10 *parts of cheese butter to 1 part chives, finely chopped*

10 *parts of cheese butter to 1 part sap cheese, grated*

DEVILED STUFFED EGGS (COLD)

6 *shelled hard-boiled eggs*	1 *tablespoon* MAYONNAISE
2 *tablespoons soft sweet*	*Pinch cayenne pepper*
butter	*Few drops Worcestershire*
1 *tablespoon cream cheese*	*sauce*
1 *teaspoon French mustard*	*Salt to taste*
1 *tablespoon English*	
mustard	

Cut the eggs in halves, lengthwise, remove the yolks; mash and mix with other ingredients. Beat with a wire whisk until the combination is light and fluffy. Spoon mixture into the egg whites; or use a pastry bag fitted with a fluted tube. Decorate each egg half with slices of pitted ripe olives or stuffed olives.

Cool in refrigerator before serving.

ANCHOVY CANAPES (HOT)

Remove anchovy filets from oil, drain thoroughly on absorbent paper napkin or cloth. Sprinkle them with 1 tablespoon of lemon juice, 1 teaspoon finely chopped onions and parsley. Toast slices of bread. Trim the crusts. Cut into finger strips wide enough to hold 2 anchovies. When the anchovy filets have been placed on the toast fingers, side by side, sprinkle them with a few drops of the marinade of lemon juice, onion, and parsley, also a little melted butter. Arrange the toast fingers on a baking sheet or piepan and heat thoroughly in a hot oven of 450° F for 4 to 5 minutes.

Serve on a napkin placed on a hot platter. Garnish with lemon and fresh crisp parsley.

ANCHOVY CANAPES (COLD)

Spread toast slices with cream cheese combined with finely cut chives. Lay overlapping filets of anchovies over the cream cheese. Trim crusts and cut into canapé size, in squares or triangles. Decorate with thin strips of red pimentos.

ROQUEFORT ON TOAST ROUNDS

Blend 2 parts of Roquefort cheese with one part of butter. When mixture is soft and creamy season with a pinch of paprika. Beat in cognac to taste. Spread mixture on toast rounds. Or use a pastry bag with a fancy tube. Decorate each round with a thin slice of ripe olive.

SHRIMP CANAPES

Spread toast rounds with butter. Lay a slice of hard-boiled egg on each. Spread egg slice with a little mayonnaise. Then arrange 2 shrimp halves on each. Garnish each round with a mayonnaise star, by using a pastry bag and star tube. Top with a thin sprig of parsley. Serve with lemon wedges.

SMOKED SALMON CANAPES

Spread slices of toast with soft cream cheese. Place slices of smoked salmon on the cream cheese. Trim crusts. Cut into desired shapes. Sprinkle with finely chopped onions mixed with finely cut chives or chopped parsley. Or decorate with slices of hard-boiled eggs or finely chopped hard-boiled eggs.

CHEESE CROUTONS [Croutons au Fromage]

(Serves 4 to 6)

1 cup grated imported
   Gruyère or Emmental
   cheese
¼ cup grated Parmesan or
   Sbrinz (See note below)
¼ cup dry white wine

2 eggs
1 teaspoon paprika
Pinch of salt
4 ounces butter
1 French bread

Combine the above ingredients—except the butter and the bread—in a mixing bowl. Blend well to form a smooth spread. Cut the French bread diagonally in ¼-inch-thick slices. Sauté in butter until slightly brown on one side. Spread the toasted sides with about 1 tablespoon of the cheese mixture, about ¼ inch thick. Dust with paprika. Place the croutons on buttered baking sheet and bake in hot 475° F oven from 5 to 6 minutes or until cheese is brown and very hot and the croutons crisp. Serve at once.

Note: Cheese croutons and a tossed salad are an ideal luncheon dish. When the croutons are served with cocktails they should be cut in smaller pieces and less cheese spread should be used.

DEVILED SARDINES SUR CROUTONS

(Serves 4 to 6)

3 cans boned skinless
   sardines
1 teaspoon French mustard
1 teaspoon English mustard
Juice of 1 lemon
Few drops Worcestershire
   sauce

Few drops Tabasco
1 egg yolk
½ cup white bread crumbs
6 slices of toast cut in the
   shape of sardines
Butter to sauté bread

Roll sardines in sauce made of French and English mustards, lemon juice, Worcestershire and Tabasco sauces, and egg yolk. Or coat each, using a brush. Then roll, one by one, in bread crumbs. Broil 3 to 4 minutes or sauté them in oil until they are golden brown. Keep hot. Sauté toast in butter. Place sardines on toast. Secure them with frilled toothpicks. Serve with lemon wedges. Garnish with water cress.

CRABMEAT REMICK (Serves 6)

1 tablespoon finely chopped shallots	Dash paprika
1 teaspoon butter	Dash cayenne
1 tablespoon sherry	Dash Worcestershire sauce
1 cup MAYONNAISE	Dash Tabasco
½ cup chili sauce	1 pound crabmeat
½ teaspoon dry mustard	2 tablespoons grated Parmesan cheese

Cook shallots in melted butter until limp, then stir in sherry. Blend with Mayonnaise, chili sauce, mustard, paprika, cayenne, Worcestershire and Tabasco sauces.

Toss crabmeat with the sauce gently so that lumps are not disturbed. Spoon into well-washed clam shells or small patty shells. Sprinkle with grated Parmesan cheese and additional paprika. Bake in a preheated 500° F (or very hot) oven for several minutes or until well browned and piping hot.

CRABMEAT EXQUISITE (Serves 6)

⅓ cup olive oil	Pinch pepper
3 tablespoons chopped shallots	1 tablespoon capers
1 clove garlic, mashed to pulp	1 tablespoon chopped anchovies
2 cups skinned and seeded ripe tomatoes, chopped fine	1 teaspoon chopped tarragon leaves
⅓ cup tarragon vinegar	2 cups MAYONNAISE
1 teaspoon salt	1 pound fresh crabmeat
	Slices hard-boiled eggs
	Slices stuffed olives

Heat olive oil in saucepan. Add chopped shallots and sauté for a few minutes. Add garlic, tomatoes, vinegar, salt, and pepper. Cook all together slowly for about 30 minutes, until reduced to smooth paste. Let cool. When mixture is cold add capers, anchovies, tarragon leaves, and Mayonnaise. Blend crabmeat into this mixture carefully and thoroughly. Serve in individual clam shells, *pâté* shells, thin tartlets, or on a large hors d'oeuvre platter. Garnish with slices of hard-boiled eggs and stuffed olives.

LOBSTER COCKTAIL GOURMET

(Serves 4)

4 *fresh crisp lettuce leaves*
1 *cup cooked lobster meat cut into ⅓-inch pieces*
2 *hard-boiled egg yolks, finely chopped*

For the cocktail sauce, mix following ingredients thoroughly and chill:

⅓ *cup* MAYONNAISE   4 *drops Tabasco*
⅓ *cup catsup*   ½ *teaspoon English mustard*
⅓ *cup chili sauce*   1 *tablespoon grated*
¼ *cup sherry wine*   *horse-radish*
2 *tablespoons lemon juice*   *Dash salt*

Line four cocktail or champagne glasses with thoroughly washed and drained lettuce leaves. Place lobster meat on the lettuce. Spoon cocktail sauce over lobster. Sprinkle with finely chopped egg yolks.

OYSTERS ROCKEFELLER

(Serves 4)

¼ *pound butter*
12 *shallots, finely chopped*
1 *clove garlic, finely chopped*
½ *bunch water cress, chopped very fine*
½ *bunch parsley, chopped very fine*
½ *pound fresh spinach, chopped very fine*
½ *cup fine bread crumbs*
4 *egg yolks*

1 *teaspoon arrowroot or cornstarch*
¼ *cup Pernod*
1 *teaspoon salt*
1 *teaspoon Worcestershire sauce*
Dash *Tabasco*
Rock *salt*
2 *dozen oysters on the half shell*
¼ *cup grated Parmesan cheese*

Heat two thirds of the butter in a large saucepan. Stir in shallots and garlic; simmer about 5 minutes, stirring frequently. Add water cress, parsley, spinach, and cook for 8 to 10 minutes or until greens are completely wilted. Remove from heat and stir in bread crumbs. Beat egg yolks slightly, add arrowroot or cornstarch and the Pernod. Stir until smooth, then blend into the vegetable mixture and cook for a minute or two, stirring briskly. Season with salt, Worcestershire and Tabasco sauces. Cool.

Pour an even layer of rock salt in a large shallow baking pan and set the oysters in the salt. Spoon an equal amount of vegetable mixture over each oyster, sprinkle with grated cheese and dribble with remaining melted butter. Bake in a preheated 450° F (or hot) oven for 8 to 10 minutes. Serve immediately.

OYSTERS CASINO

(Serves 4)

Rock salt
2 dozen oysters on the
  half shell
6 strips bacon
½ cup finely chopped
  green pepper
¼ cup finely chopped
  pimento

½ pound butter, softened
Juice of 2 lemons
1 teaspoon Worcestershire
  sauce
Dash Tabasco

Put a level bed of salt in a large shallow baking pan. Place oysters firmly on the salt to hold them in place during baking.

Cut bacon into pieces about 1½ inches in length. Fry for several minutes but not long enough to crisp the meat. Drain and set aside. Cook green pepper in a little of the bacon fat until limp. Cool, then blend together thoroughly with pimento, butter, lemon juice, Worcestershire and Tabasco sauces. Spoon some of this butter mixture over each oyster and place a piece of bacon on top. Bake in a preheated 400° F (or moderately hot) oven for 8 to 10 minutes. Serve bubbling hot.

CALVES' BRAINS VINAIGRETTE

(Serves 4)

2 pairs calves' brains
1 small head of lettuce,
  shredded
1 cup vinaigrette sauce

1 tablespoon chopped
  parsley
Water cress

Cook brains according to directions given for CALVES' BRAINS AU BEURRE NOIR. When cool, pat dry with paper towels.

Split brains in half and arrange on a bed of shredded lettuce. Spoon on vinaigrette sauce, sprinkle with chopped parsley, and garnish with water cress.

EGGS AND CAVIAR WITH VEGETABLE SALAD
[*Eggs à la Russe*]

(Serves 4)

1½ cups Vegetable Salad	1 cup MAYONNAISE
Lettuce leaves	1 ounce caviar
8 hard-boiled eggs, shelled and halved lengthwise	Water cress

To prepare the Vegetable Salad:

Cook limited equal quantities of fresh vegetables, such as carrots, turnips, peas, lima beans, string beans, in slightly salted water until barely tender. Let cool. Drain well. Then combine vegetables with about 3 tablespoons of Mayonnaise, a few drops of Worcestershire sauce, a pinch of white pepper, and a pinch of salt.

Arrange lettuce leaves in a serving bowl or on individual plates. Spoon the vegetable salad over the lettuce leaves. Set the egg halves, cut side up, on top of the vegetable salad. Spoon the Mayonnaise over the eggs so it covers them and the vegetables. Place caviar in middle of each mayonnaised egg half. Garnish platter or individual plates with bouquet of water cress.

Soups

We have come a long way in our cuisine since the days, not so long ago, when canned tomato soup, with no seasoning added and a blob of whipped cream bobbing on top, was considered a most elegant first course.

We still, unfortunately, are prone to identify soup with cans or packages of dehydrated powder or flakes. Many of these products are of undoubted excellence. Some of them provide a splendid base from which, with a little imagination, it is a simple matter to go on to better things, such as GERMINY SOUP.

Also, many canned and dehydrated soups can be used for stock; the beef broths and consommés for beef stock, the chicken broths for chicken stock, and the bottled clam juice for fish stock. Stock, the basis of sauces and gravies, seems fraught with mystery to those inexperienced in cookery. It is, very simply, the strong broth that results when meat, bones, vegetables, and seasonings are cooked together, long and slowly.

Whether a soup should be a clear soup, a cream soup, a richer bisque, or something heartier depends upon whether it is to be an appetizer for a dinner or, together with a salad and a dessert, to constitute an entire meal.

Louis XIV of France used to insist that several tureens of soup be presented to him at dinner, so he might have a choice. Invariably, however, when the lids of the tureens were lifted he is said to have been unable to resist any one of the aromas and to have drunk all of them!

Clear soups, like broths or consommés or, for those who are feeling luxurious, a green turtle soup with sherry, are appetizer soups. After a predinner wine or cocktails, canapés and hors d'oeuvres, they freshen the mouth and stimulate the palate for the fish, poultry, or meat that follows.

In warm weather, cold soups such as VICHYSSOISE, jellied chicken broth, tomato madrilène, iced consommé or broth are refreshing and appetizing.

A main-course soup might be LENTIL SOUP LONGCHAMPS with frankfurter slices and sherry, a black-bean soup, or a strong consommé with little meatballs. And never let us forget the delicious chowders—clam, oyster, corn, lobster, shrimp, and all the others—that have come down to us from our ancestors, many of them from New England. Or the delicious gumbos we inherit from the French and Spanish settlers of the South, especially from Louisiana.

Longchamps' executive chef, Ernest Imhof, and I have chosen with the greatest care the easily prepared soup recipes that follow. We promise any one of them will be fine fare, especially if served in a lidded marmite bowl that holds the heat, accompanied by a crusty loaf of toasted garlic, cheese, or herbed bread.

Soup, like all food, tastes better when it has visual appeal, if, after it is ladled into tureen, bowl, cup, or soup plate, it is garnished with chopped parsley, paprika, croutons, snipped chives, grated cheese, or served with noodles, vegetables, rice, or tapioca that have been cooked separately—whichever offers a contrast in color and is a complement to taste.

GERMINY SOUP

(Serves 8)

8 *cups chicken consommé*   ½ *teaspoon salt*
8 *egg yolks*   ½ *pound sorrel* (See note
3 *cups heavy cream*   below)
4 *tablespoons butter*

Heat consommé to the boiling point. Combine egg yolks and cream in a bowl and mix thoroughly. Beat a little of the hot consommé into egg-cream mixture, then beat this into remaining hot consommé. Cook over a low heat, stirring constantly, until soup thickens slightly. Do not boil. Add 3 tablespoons butter and ½ teaspoon salt. Set aside.

Snip off thick sorrel stems and discard. Chop leaves quite fine and heat in the remaining tablespoon of butter until slightly wilted. Stir into soup and serve immediately.

Note: If sorrel is not available in your neighborhood use the same amount of spinach or water cress. For those who are fond of the flavor of sorrel the amount can be doubled.

CHICKEN GUMBO A LA CREOLE

(Serves 6)

2 *tablespoons butter*   2 *tablespoons uncooked rice*
1 *large onion, chopped*   ¼ *pound okra* (or ½
1 *stalk celery, chopped fine*   *package frozen), sliced*
2 *leeks, chopped fine*   2 *ripe tomatoes, skinned*
1 *green pepper, chopped*   *and diced*
   fine   1 *teaspoon salt*
½ *cup diced cooked ham*   ¼ *teaspoon pepper*
2 *raw chicken legs, skinned,*   *Chopped parsley*
   boned, diced
1½ *quarts chicken broth,*
   canned or homemade

Melt butter in a large saucepan. Toss in onions, celery, leeks, green pepper; cook over a low heat, stirring frequently, for about 10 minutes. Add ham and chicken; cook 5 minutes. Pour in broth, cook to a boil, then reduce heat and simmer gently for 30 minutes. Stir in rice, simmer another 15 minutes. Finally, add okra and tomatoes; cook 5 more minutes. Season with salt and pepper to taste. Serve with chopped parsley scattered on top.

OLD-FASHIONED CREAM OF CHICKEN SOUP

(Serves 6 to 8)

½ cup butter	Dash white pepper
1 onion, chopped fine	2 quarts chicken broth,
2 leeks, white part only,	canned or homemade
chopped fine	1 cup light cream
1 small bay leaf	2 egg yolks
1 stalk celery, chopped fine	½ cup cooked diced chicken
½ cup flour	¼ cup cooked rice
1 teaspoon salt	¼ cup cooked diced celery

Heat butter in a saucepan. Stir in onion, leeks, bay leaf, celery; cook over a low heat, stirring frequently, for about 10 minutes. Do not allow to brown. Add flour and salt and pepper; blend well. Pour in broth, cook to a boil, stirring continuously, then reduce heat and simmer gently for 1½ to 2 hours.

Strain into another saucepan and heat to a boil. Heat cream until a film shines on the surface; beat egg yolks lightly. Gradually beat cream into egg yolks, then add mixture to soup. Heat through but don't boil or soup will curdle. Just before serving, stir in cooked chicken, rice, and celery.

GREEN PEA SOUP LONGCHAMPS

(Serves 6)

1½ cups dried green split
  peas
¼ pound butter, divided
1 carrot, sliced thin
1 medium onion, sliced thin
1 stalk celery, sliced thin
2 leeks, sliced thin
1 ham bone or ham hock
1 tablespoon flour
1 teaspoon salt

¼ teaspoon pepper
¼ teaspoon sugar
2 quarts broth, chicken or
  beef, homemade or
  canned
½ cup light cream
½ cup cooked vermicelli
Small cubes bread,
  browned in butter

Soak peas overnight. Next morning, drain, cover with fresh water, and cook for about 15 minutes. Drain again.

Melt half the butter in a kettle. Toss in sliced vegetables and ham bone or hock, cook over a low heat for about 10 minutes, stirring frequently. Add peas and stir in the flour, salt, pepper, and sugar. Pour in broth and cook to a boil. Cover, reduce heat and simmer gently for 1½ to 2 hours. Remove from heat and work mixture through a sieve. Chop any ham left on the bone and add to soup. Bring soup to a boil again, skim if necessary, and taste to see if more salt is needed. Just before serving, stir in cream and remaining butter. Add vermicelli and serve with browned bread cubes.

MINESTRONE MILANAISE

(Serves 8)

¼ cup dry white beans
1 stalk celery
2 leeks
2 large onions
2 carrots
½ small head of cabbage
½ pound green beans
½ cup fresh peas
2 cloves garlic
¼ cup salad oil
2 large ripe tomatoes,
    skinned and diced

½ cup tomato sauce or 1
    tablespoon tomato purée
1½ quarts homemade beef
    broth or 5 cans
    (10½-ounce size) beef
    broth
1 cup spaghetti, broken
    into pieces
Few sprigs parsley, chopped
Grated Parmesan cheese

Soak the beans in cold water overnight. Wash vegetables; cut celery, leeks, onions, carrots, cabbage in extremely thin slices; trim off ends of green beans and cut in small pieces; shell peas and chop garlic fine.

Heat oil in a large kettle, stir in chopped vegetables and dry white beans; sauté over moderate heat, stirring constantly to prevent sticking, for about 10 minutes. Add tomatoes, tomato sauce or purée, and simmer 5 minutes longer. Pour in broth, bring to a boil, and cook gently for 1 hour. Toss in spaghetti and cook 15 minutes more. Add salt if necessary (sometimes canned beef broth is quite salty).

Serve with parsley and grated cheese on top.

LENTIL SOUP LONGCHAMPS

(Serves 6 generously)

1 box (1 pound) lentils
4 tablespoons butter
6 strips bacon, cut in pieces
2 medium onions, diced fine
1 stalk celery, diced fine
2 leeks, diced fine
1 clove garlic, minced
1½ quarts beef broth (See
note below)

2 medium-size raw
potatoes, cubed
1 teaspoon salt
Pinch pepper
4 frankfurters, sliced thin
Chopped parsley

Soak the lentils in cold water overnight. The following day, when you are ready to prepare the soup, melt butter in a large, heavy skillet; add the bacon, onions, celery, leeks, and garlic. Sauté over moderate heat for about 20 minutes or until vegetables have taken on a little color. Give the mixture an occasional stir. Add drained lentils and cook together for a few minutes more. Then transfer to a large kettle, add the broth and cook slowly for an hour, or until lentils are tender. At this point add cubed potatoes, salt, and pepper. Cook another 15 minutes. Just before serving, stir in the thinly sliced frankfurters and heat thoroughly. Shower with chopped parsley before serving. This is naturally a thick soup but if it seems too thick for you add a little scalded cream or additional broth. Have a decanter of sherry on the table for those who wish to add a little to their soup.

Note: If you do not wish to make the beef broth use 4 cans (10½-ounce size) beef broth.

MANHATTAN CLAM CHOWDER

(Serves 6 to 8)

30 *chowder clams*
2 *tablespoons butter*
2 *onions, chopped coarsely*
1 *stalk celery, finely diced*
2 *green peppers, seeded,*
   finely diced
2 *leeks, finely chopped*
3 *large tomatoes, peeled*
   and diced small
2 *pounds potatoes, peeled*
   and diced small

Bouquet garni: *Few sprigs*
   parsley, celery leaves, 2
   bay leaves all tied together
1 *teaspoon dried thyme*
Pinch *cayenne pepper*
2 *teaspoons salt*
2 *tablespoons chili sauce*
Dash *Tabasco*
1 *teaspoon arrowroot*
Chopped *parsley*

Add thoroughly washed clams to 2 quarts of water and bring to a boil. Reduce heat and continue cooking 10 to 12 minutes. Drain, strain the broth and reserve. Discard clam shells and cut clams into small pieces, removing necks and membranes. Melt butter in a large kettle. Stir in onions and cook over a brisk heat until light brown. Add celery, green peppers, leeks and continue cooking until limp. Now stir in tomatoes, potatoes, and clam broth. Bring to a boil, skim off any froth, and drop in the *bouquet garni*. Season with thyme, cayenne, salt, chili sauce, Tabasco; simmer over a low heat for about 30 minutes.

Remove *bouquet garni* and discard. Make a smooth paste of arrowroot and a little water. Stir into chowder and cook, stirring constantly, until slightly thick. Just before serving, stir in clams and chopped parsley.

FRENCH ONION SOUP

(Makes 2 quarts)

¼ pound butter	Salt
2½ pounds onions, minced fine	Pepper
	Croutons of French bread
1 tablespoon flour	
2 quarts broth or consommé, homemade or canned	

Melt butter in a saucepan. Add onions and cook over a low heat, stirring frequently, until golden brown and tender. Stir in flour and continue cooking 5 to 6 minutes longer.

Add boiling broth or consommé and cook 15 to 20 minutes. Season to taste with salt and pepper. Serve with nicely browned croutons of French bread.

VICHYSSOISE

(Serves 6)

4 tablespoons butter	Pinch white pepper
2 leeks, sliced	Pinch nutmeg
2 stalks celery, sliced	Few drops Maggi Seasoning
1 medium onion, sliced	1 cup heavy cream
2 pounds potatoes, sliced	1 bundle chives, chopped
1 quart chicken stock	(See note below)
1 teaspoon salt	

Melt butter in a saucepan. Add leeks (make sure they are washed free of sand), celery, onion; cook over a low heat for about 10 minutes, stirring frequently. *Do not let these vegetables brown.*

Add potatoes, pour in chicken stock, and cook to a boil. Reduce heat, cover and cook 40 to 50 minutes or until potatoes are very tender. Work mixture through a strainer or blend in an electric blender. Cool, then stir in salt, pepper, nutmeg, Maggi Seasoning, and cream. Serve very cold with a sprinkling of chopped chives on top. If you prefer a thinner Vichyssoise, stir in a little extra cream.

Note: Frozen chopped chives may be used.

BOUILLABAISSE

(Serves 6 to 8)

¼ cup of oil

2 onions, sliced thin

4 leeks, white parts, washed, sliced thin

1 stalk of celery, ribs peeled washed thoroughly and sliced fine

2 fennels, washed and sliced fine

6 cloves garlic, peeled, crushed

2 bay leaves

½ teaspoon saffron

½ teaspoon thyme

4 large tomatoes, peeled, seeded, cut coarsely

Salt and pepper

2 1½-pound lobsters cut into 1-inch pieces

24 mussels, scraped and thoroughly washed

1 glass of white wine

2½ to 3 pounds salt-water fish cut in pieces (red snapper, English sole, turbot, halibut—whatever available)

12 shrimp, shells removed and deveined

12 sea scallops

2 quarts of fish stock from fish bones and trimmings (See note below)

2 tablespoons coarsely chopped parsley

Large slices of French bread, rubbed with garlic and browned golden brown in oil

Heat the oil in large enough skillet to hold all ingredients; add the thin-sliced onions, leeks, celery, and fennels and sauté over low flame for 15 to 20 minutes; add garlic, bay leaves, saffron, thyme, tomatoes, salt and pepper. Add lobster pieces, mussels, and white wine; cover and let cook 5 minutes, then add all other fish.

Pour in fish stock, bring to boil and let cook 10 minutes. Transfer fish and shellfish carefully from skillet into serving bowl. Cook the soup 10 to 15 minutes, season to taste and pour over the fish.

Sprinkle with coarsely chopped parsley and serve piping hot with the croutons on a separate dish.

Note: Canned or bottled clam juice may be substituted for fish stock.

Eggs

The egg, in or out of its shell, is a thing of beauty. In its shell it, a symbol of life, has been elemental in design since the earliest days. Out of its shell it is an almost perfect food.

Among the countless egg dishes that cooks have been inspired to concoct, directions for several of which are given in this chapter, the omelette remains most popular. I think this is because it has never been improved upon.

Omelette pans were found in the ruins of the pleasure-loving city of Pompeii. Louis XV of France had a kitchen set up in the royal apartments at the palace of Versailles so he might prepare omelettes for his Du Barry. And Mme. Poulard, of Mont-Saint-Michel, attained world-wide fame because of the delectable omelettes she used to prepare when a boatload of sight-seers to the historic abbey would descend, often unexpectedly, upon her hotel. Her hungry visitors used to watch, admiringly but impatiently, as she knelt at her hearth, constantly moving her omelette pan, with its slanting sides and long handle, back and forth over the glowing fire. And always these visitors went home to the four corners of the earth, singing her praise.

Sometimes, after salting and peppering her egg mixture, Mme. Poulard would add chopped herbs or grated cheese. Or, just before she was ready to fold an omelette, she would spoon onto it minced ham, mushroom slices, minced chicken, chicken livers, crisp bacon, tomatoes, anchovies, or whatever else her hotel's limited larder might afford.

Omelette *aficionados* guard their pans—as salad *aficionados* guard their bowls—from water and wipe them clean with paper so they will retain an oiled surface.

There are those who prefer to use water in an omelette mixture rather than milk or cream, insisting this makes for a more delicate texture. At Longchamps we add neither milk nor water.

Some believe six eggs are the limit that should be prepared at one time. Others raise the number to ten or lower it to three or four. My chefs choose to make individual omelettes of three eggs each—in piping-hot pans which are coated with butter that sizzles but does not brown.

Only upon the need for good butter and fresh eggs is there no difference of opinion.

The best eggs in the market are marked AA or A. They, with firmer whites and yolks, are excellent for poaching, coddling, baking, boiling, frying. However, B and C eggs, although their whites and yolks are thinner and their shells quicker to break, contain the same food value as the AA's and A's.

Eggs are heaviest when they are fresh. Because an egg shell is porous some very small portion of the water content evaporates each day.

OMELETTES

Note: To make an omelette requires practice. It should be mellow inside, oval in shape, plump in the middle, pointed at the ends, and golden in color.

The main point is to work rapidly. At first, try making an individual omelette with two eggs only. Always the fewer eggs used the easier an omelette is to handle.

Break the eggs into a bowl and beat thoroughly.

Season with salt and pepper.

Place a tablespoon of butter in a frying pan and let it heat, but not brown, over a high heat.

Pour the egg mixture into the pan.

Stir the eggs with a fork for a few seconds while shaking the pan.

When the eggs begin to thicken fold the edges toward the center.

Have a hot plate ready and when the eggs are cooked slide them, from the side away from you, to it.

If you are preparing a stuffed omelette, have the filling ready beforehand. When the eggs begin to set place the filling on them and fold one side over carefully to form a pouch. Let the omelette slide to the side of the pan, again away from you, and slip it gently to a hot plate.

OMELETTE WITH FINE HERBS

(Serves 2)

4 eggs, well beaten
Season with salt and pepper
1½ tablespoons mixed herbs (chopped parsley, finely cut chives, and tarragon)

Proceed according to directions for a plain omelette.

COUNTRY-STYLE OMELETTE

(Serves 2)

2 tablespoons of butter
4 mushrooms, washed and sliced thin
1 small onion, finely chopped
2 strips bacon, cut fine
1 medium-size cooked potato, cubed

Salt and pepper
1 tablespoon fine herbs (chopped parsley and chives)
4 eggs

Melt half the butter in a skillet. Add the sliced mushrooms and sauté over a low fire for a few minutes, then add the onions, bacon, and potatoes. Sauté all 2 or 3 minutes longer.

Remove from the heat, let cool a little before adding the fine herbs. Combine the above ingredients with beaten eggs and proceed to make the omelette with the remaining butter according to directions for a plain omelette.

STUFFED OMELETTE MASCOTTE

(Serves 2)

4 artichoke bottoms, cooked and diced	4 eggs
	Salt
1½ tablespoons butter	Pepper
1½ tablespoons BASIC CREAM SAUCE	

Sauté, lightly, minced artichokes in ¾ tablespoons of butter, then stir in the Cream Sauce.

Beat and season eggs and cook with the remaining butter in usual way. When eggs begin to set place the artichoke mixture on them. Fold omelette over the artichoke mixture and, when it is ready, slide it onto a hot platter.

Garnish with crisp water-cress bouquet.

STUFFED OMELETTE WITH CREAMED CHICKEN AND MUSHROOMS A LA REINE

(Serves 2)

½ cup diced chicken leftovers	1½ tablespoons BASIC CREAM SAUCE
4 large cooked mushrooms, diced	4 eggs
	Salt
1½ tablespoons butter	Pepper

Proceed as for Omelette Mascotte, using chicken and mushrooms in creamed sauce instead of the artichokes.

OMELETTE PANCAKE STYLE

(Serves 2)

1 *tablespoon of butter*
4 *eggs, well beaten*
Salt and pepper to taste

Heat the butter in a frying pan about 6 inches in diameter. Combine the eggs, salt, and pepper; pour into the pan. Stir slowly with a fork, shaking the pan once or twice. After the eggs begin to thicken let stand for a moment without stirring so eggs may take on color at the bottom. Sprinkle a little melted butter around the sides of the pan. Be sure the omelette is loosened on the pan. Turn upside down on a *hot plate!*

To introduce variety, add any one of the following to the basic mixture:

Fermière (farm wife)

4 medium-size mushrooms, sliced thin, sautéed in butter, 2 tablespoons well-drained, cooked, chopped spinach, 1 small onion, chopped and cooked in butter, 1 teaspoon finely cut chives.

Country Style

Sliced bacon, diced potatoes, chopped smothered onion, and chopped parsley.

Ménagère (thrifty wife)

Finely sliced beef leftovers combined with some chopped green pepper and onions, sautéed until tender in butter.

Suissesse (Swiss style)

Diced Swiss cheese, grated cheese with a tablespoon of unsweetened whipped cream.

Lenten

Asparagus tips cut in half-inch lengths, Julienne of well-drained cooked spinach, smothered chopped onions, and diced pimento.

Tyrolienne (*Tyrol mountain style*)

Spoon stewed fresh tomato in the center and top with some French-fried onions.

Forestière (*of the forest*)

Thinly sliced mushrooms sautéed in butter and freshly chopped fine herbs.

SCRAMBLED EGGS WITH CHICKEN LIVERS

(Serves 3)

9 *eggs*	*Salt and pepper to taste*
3 *tablespoons cream*	3 *tablespoons sweet butter*

Beat the eggs well with a fork. Then, gradually, beat in 2 tablespoons cream, salt and pepper. Heat 2 tablespoons of the butter in skillet, add the egg mixture and cook over low heat, stirring with wooden spoon to keep the eggs smooth and free from lumps. Remove pan from the heat before eggs are completely set. Stir in remaining cream and sweet butter.

CHICKEN-LIVER MIXTURE

1 *tablespoon butter*	*Salt and pepper to taste*
12 *chicken livers, cut in two*	3 *tablespoons beef gravy*
1 *tablespoon chopped parsley*	or TOMATO SAUCE

Heat butter in a skillet. Add the livers and cook until they are brown, but not dry. Add the parsley and salt and pepper.

Then add beef gravy or Tomato Sauce and reheat mixture slightly. Do not let it come to boil.

Put the livers on a plate and surround them with the scrambled eggs.

POACHED EGGS AND HAM IN ASPIC

(Serves 6)

4 *cups rich beef broth,* *homemade or canned*
2 *to 3 ripe tomatoes, finely* *chopped*
1 *onion, sliced*
1 *carrot, sliced*
2 *stalks celery, sliced*
Few sprigs parsley
3 *to 4 peppercorns*

3 *egg whites, beaten*
5 *envelopes unflavored* *gelatin*
¼ *cup Madeira, sherry, or* *cognac*
Tarragon or water-cress *sprigs*
6 *eggs, poached*
6 *small slices cooked ham*

Combine beef broth, tomatoes, onion, carrot, celery, parsley, peppercorns, egg whites, and gelatin in a saucepan and cook to a boil, stirring constantly. Simmer gently for 20 to 30 minutes. Remove from heat and strain through a cheesecloth. Stir in Madeira, sherry, or cognac; cool.

When aspic is cold but still liquid, spoon a thin layer in 6 individual molds or custard cups (or a large 1½-quart mold). Chill in refrigerator until firm. Now dip tarragon or watercress sprigs in the liquid aspic and decorate bottoms of molds. Chill again. When firm spoon on another layer and chill a third time. Meanwhile, trim edges of poached eggs so they will fit into molds, then place on the aspic with a layer of ham on top. Fill mold with aspic and again refrigerate until firm. To serve: turn mold upside down on a cold serving platter and garnish with bouquets of water cress and tomato wedges.

FRENCH BAKED EGGS AND ONIONS
(Serves 6)

4 *tablespoons butter*	*Pepper*
4 *medium onions, thinly sliced*	3 *tablespoons butter*
	3 *tablespoons flour*
12 *hard-cooked eggs, thinly sliced*	2 *cups light cream, heated*
Salt	3 *tablespoons grated Swiss or Parmesan cheese*

Melt 4 tablespoons butter in a large, heavy skillet, add the sliced onions and cook over a low heat for 10 minutes or so. Onions should be soft but not brown. Butter a medium-size baking dish and layer the eggs and onions, alternately, starting with eggs. Sprinkle a little salt and pepper between the layers.

Melt the 3 tablespoons of butter in a saucepan, stir in the flour, and cook for a minute or two, stirring constantly. Do not brown. Then stir in the hot cream and cook, stirring constantly, over moderate heat until sauce has thickened—8 to 10 minutes. Pour sauce over the eggs and onions, sprinkle top with grated cheese, dot with a few bits of butter, and bake in a 400° F (or moderately hot) oven until top of casserole has turned golden.

A handsome and delicious luncheon or supper dish.

POACHED EGGS FLORENTINE (Serves 4)

2 *cups cooked, buttered spinach, seasoned with salt and pepper*	¼ *cup grated Swiss cheese (or half Parmesan and half Swiss)*
8 *poached eggs*	2 *tablespoons of melted butter*
2 *cups* MORNAY SAUCE	

Cover bottom of buttered baking dish with cooked spinach. Lay the eggs on the spinach. Cover with Mornay Sauce and

sprinkle with grated cheese and the melted butter. Bake in a
hot oven of 425° F just long enough to brown the topping.
Care should be taken not to overcook the eggs.

POACHED EGGS BENEDICT

(Serves 4)

White vinegar	1½ *cups* HOLLANDAISE SAUCE
8 *poached eggs*	8 *slices of truffles*
4 *English muffins*	(optional)
8 *slices ham*	

Half fill a wide and shallow saucepan with boiling water.
Add 2 tablespoons of white vinegar to each quart of water
used. No salt please. Break the eggs, gently, one by one, into
the boiling water-vinegar mixture. Meanwhile, split, toast,
and butter the muffins and broil 8 slices of ham. Also poach
eggs 2 to 3 minutes, or until whites are firm. On each muffin
half place one slice of broiled ham and one poached egg. Top
with Hollandaise Sauce and garnish, if desired, with sliced
truffles.

Cheese

We read of poor poets and artists who live in attics on bread, cheese, and wine. Attics, I have no doubt, are more romantic in books than they are in reality. But I can never quite bring myself to feel sorry for the man or woman who lives on the crusty dark bread that is prevalent in France and Italy, where most poets and artists choose to struggle, an honest cheese and a modest fresh wine.

I said *honest cheese!* This rules out the rubbery processed products and the slippery dips and spreads which have no right to be called cheese, since they bear no family resemblance to any one of the four hundred and more cheese varieties.

My wife sometimes feels constrained to ask: "But why do you get so excited about the 'rubbery and slippery' products? You neither eat them at home nor buy them for your restaurants." She is right, of course.

Actually it is not the products themselves I deplore, only that they are known as cheese. I find this an affront to the tradition of cheese making and to the respectful consideration that cheese receives from those concerned with each and every step of its production.

On the Longchamps cheeseboards, on which all cheese has been brought to room temperature, as it should be, patrons are certain to find an oblong of Emmenthaler from Switzerland, with many eyes of about the same size, all eloquently moist with rich ripeness.

Beside this Swiss cheese there will be a round, crusted Brie from France, made as painstakingly today as it was five hundred years ago when the father of Louis XII sent Bries as New Year's presents. Our chefs are careful to have this delicate cheese, which must be neither too young nor too old, removed from the refrigerator just in time for it to reach its ideal creamy consistency for the luncheon or the dinner hour.

There also will be a Camembert, honored, as it should be, in the French village of Camembert with a statue of Mme. Harel, the farmer's wife, who was its originator way back around the late eighteenth century.

Of course there's a Roquefort, made from ewe's milk mixed with bread crumbs, impregnated with a greenish mold and ripened in the damp limestone caves of the French town whose name it bears.

And need I add there will be a fine ivory-colored, napkin-wrapped Stilton. Always when I see a patron scooping into a Stilton, I have a sense of satisfaction. I know the rich aroma that rises from it. For, likely, it was I who poured the sherry or the port over it; slowly, so it would soak through every blue-streaked inch of it.

In the Longchamps kitchens the Italian Parmesan which, when it is aged, is the hardest cheese in the world, is my choice for the grating cheese used for soups, sauces, *pasta*, eggs, and *au gratin* dishes.

I am fortunate in the amount of cheese I can buy. For, up to a certain point, the bigger the wheel the better the cheese. Only when a wheel is very much oversize does cheese have a tendency to deteriorate.

I import cheese only when it has not been satisfactorily duplicated in this country. I buy many domestic cheeses.

We have made cheddar in the United States—and made it well—ever since our colonial days. Many American cheddars are identified with the name of the state from which they come. All of them are known, less formally, as store cheese, yellow cheese, rat cheese, and bar cheese, the latter, of course, because platters of it, cut into cubes, were a mainstay of pre-Prohibition's free-lunch counters.

I seriously doubt that anyone could tell the difference between a Port du Salut out of Milwaukee, where it is faithfully made according to the old and once-secret Trappist formula, or a Port du Salut out of a monastery.

We also make an excellent blue cheese, which might be called a kissing cousin of Roquefort. It, too, is impregnated with bread and mold and ripened in caves. Blue cheese is effective for many things. But serve it with a pear, stuff celery with it, or eat it on a roll or biscuit and it lacks Roquefort's indescribable texture and flavor.

Noteworthy, too, are the many cheeses that have originated in the United States.

As long ago as 1845 what is, basically, a cheddar cheese was manufactured in New England in the form of a pineapple, the symbol of hospitality.

There is our Vermont sage, just what it claims to be. And very good too.

Especially notable is our Liederkranz. For this we owe thanks to a young upstate New York delicatessen proprietor by the name of Emil Frey. Emil sought to please the members of a Liederkranz singing club by duplicating a German cheese to which they were partial. He had many failures. But he persevered until he produced a cheese very like the German importation. Romantically he called it Crown of Song, the English translation of Liederkranz. But this name lasted no longer than it took his cheese to become popular and the customers who crowded into his little store—understandably self-conscious about asking for half a pound of Crown of Song—to order the cheese by its German name.

Cheese is a complement to a variety of foods as well as a basic ingredient of a variety of popular dishes for which recipes follow.

A few years ago I spent one of the memorable days of my life at the cheese market in Holland. As I walked from display to display, eating the approved gingerbread to cleanse and prepare my mouth for the next tasting, I had no quarrel with the early Greeks who believed that cheese originated with the Gods.

SWISS CHEESE FONDUE [*Fondue Neuchâteloise*]

(Serves 6)

1½ pounds imported Swiss
   cheese
4 teaspoons cornstarch
1 clove garlic
1 cup dry white wine,
   preferably Neuchâtel

3 tablespoons kirsch
½ teaspoon salt
Dash pepper
Dash nutmeg
French bread, cut in
   bite-size cubes

Make the fondue in a flameproof earthenware casserole or a heavy pan that can be placed over an alcohol lamp.

Shred the cheese and combine thoroughly with cornstarch. Rub the inside of the cooking utensil with a cut clove of garlic. Pour in the wine and heat over a low fire until barely bubbling. Stir in the cheese-cornstarch mixture. Cook over a low heat, stirring constantly, until mixture is thick and creamy. Add kirsch, salt, pepper, and nutmeg. Remove from fire and place over an alcohol lamp. Spear cubes of bread with a fork and dip into the hot fondue.

CHEESE SOUFFLE

(Serves 4)

¼ cup butter
½ cup flour
1¾ cups milk, heated
¼ teaspoon salt
Pinch of nutmeg

½ cup grated Swiss cheese
¼ cup grated Parmesan
   cheese
5 eggs, separated

Melt the butter over a low heat. Blend in flour smoothly. Cook a few minutes, stirring constantly. But do not brown. Add the hot milk gradually, stirring all the while, and cook until smooth and thick. Take off the heat and stir in salt, nutmeg, and both the grated cheeses until thoroughly mixed. Allow mixture to cool somewhat. Then beat in the egg yolks, one at a time. Make sure the egg yolks and the other ingredients are thoroughly blended. You can, if desirable, do all this ahead of time and allow the mixture to stand until you are ready to finish and bake it.

Beat the egg whites in a generous-size bowl until they stand in peaks when lifted with the beater. Add the egg-yolk mixture, folding it into the egg whites with a wooden spoon. Make sure all white patches disappear by gently but thoroughly reaching down into the bottom of the bowl.

Pour into a well-buttered, medium-size soufflé dish (or any straight-sided casserole) and bake in a 375° F (or moderate oven) for 35 to 40 minutes or until soufflé has puffed and turned a delicate brown on top. A soufflé, when perfectly cooked, will be slightly runny when you first plunge into it but will go on cooking in its own heat right at the table. Serve the instant it comes out of the oven because, like all soufflés, it will begin to fall as it cools.

CHEESE AND BACON TART [*Quiche Lorraine*]

(Serves 4 to 6)

PASTRY:

1 cup sifted all-purpose
  flour
1 teaspoon salt
2 tablespoons shortening

2 tablespoons butter
4 to 5 tablespoons ice water
  (See note below)

FILLING:

6 strips bacon
2 large onions, minced
½ cup grated imported
  Swiss cheese
½ cup grated Parmesan
  cheese

3 whole eggs
2 egg yolks
1 teaspoon salt
2 cups milk

To make pastry: Sift flour and salt together in a bowl. Work shortening and butter into the flour with pastry blender or two knives, until mixture looks mealy. Sprinkle in 1 tablespoon of ice water at a time and mix together, lightly, with a fork. Then work the dough with your hands until it holds together. Chill thoroughly before rolling.

To roll pastry: Place on a lightly floured board. Roll dough a few strokes to flatten. Then roll lightly from center to edge until about ⅛ inch thick.

Line bottom and sides of a 9-inch piepan, pressing dough down and around evenly. Crimp the edge. Prick the bottom of pastry all over with a fork. Chill in refrigerator, if possible overnight.

Note: Or use one package of pastry mix according to package directions. This produces an adequate but less rich pastry.

To make the filling: Cut the bacon across in strips (julienne) and sauté slightly. Drain on paper towels. Sauté minced onion in bacon fat until translucent.

Sprinkle bacon over bottom of pastry, then the onion, and finally the two cheeses.

Beat 3 whole eggs plus 2 yolks with salt until well mixed, then mix in the milk.

Pour mixture into pie shell and bake in preheated 400° F (or hot) oven for 25 to 30 minutes or until a knife inserted in center of custard comes out clean. Serve hot.

WELSH RAREBIT

(Serves 4)

½ cup beer
1 tablespoon butter
1 pound cheddar cheese, cut into small pieces or grated
Salt to taste
½ teaspoon English mustard, diluted with a little beer

½ teaspoon Worcestershire sauce
2 egg yolks, mixed with 1 tablespoon of port wine or sherry
8 freshly made and trimmed triangles of toast
Paprika

In a skillet heat the beer and the butter. When beer and butter are hot, add the cheese. Stir with fork until cheese is completely melted and boiling. Season with salt, mustard, and Worcestershire sauce. Remove from fire. Stir in egg yolks and port wine or sherry and return to fire. Allow mixture to bubble for a second. Pour over hot-toast triangles. Sprinkle with paprika and serve piping hot.

A *Golden Buck* is a Welsh Rarebit with each portion topped with a poached egg.

Fish and Shellfish

Fish, which rapidly loses quality and flavor after it is taken from the water, should be three things: Fresh! FRESH!! FRESH!!!

To the restaurateurs or the housewives with pride in their kitchens a good fish dealer is essential. He should be a man who, appreciating the need for fish to be fresh, goes every day to market; knows how a fish should be cleaned, boned, cut into steaks or fileted; and, gladly, will advise on the fish that is in season—and, so, offers the most, food and flavorwise, when it costs the least.

Very rarely can a chain store or supermarket supply fish at its delectable freshest. Too much time is consumed in transportation.

Fish that has been out of the water only a short time retains much of its natural color. A freshly caught red snapper, for instance, is a handsome and dramatic thing to see. I remember a big twenty-pounder I found at the fish market one morning, so fresh it looked as if it might swim right out of the proud dealer's hands. It even smelled fresh, as fish should. Its gills were a brilliant scarlet, its scales, which lay close to its body and were slightly sticky, were a deep pink, its eyes were prominent and bright and its flesh was firm to the touch. A few hours later when this fish was delivered, boned, and cut into steaks and filets, my chefs exclaimed with delight. So did the fish-lovers among our clientele when it was served to them grilled with grapefruit sections.

If there are cries of dismay when fish appears on your table, something is wrong. Either your dealer is not giving you fish fresh enough to have its natural subtlety of flavor or whoever is cook in your house isn't preparing it as gently as good fish cookery requires.

I have found that those who associate fish with fast days

incline to having a prejudice about it that finds them cooking it with less interest and imagination than they usually manifest.

I often speculate what would happen should fish, with its protein, vitamin, and mineral content, be banned on fast days. I strongly suspect—man being essentially a contrary creature—it would become so desirable that prices would soar.

Fish is versatile—just how versatile is shown by the recipes on the succeeding pages.

The garnishes used on fish are important.

Hot fish may be garnished with small, boiled potatoes that have been sprinkled with parsley or paprika or both and broiled tomatoes that have been blessed with a touch of salt and thyme. Or slivered almonds, toasted brown in butter. Or little green nosegays of fresh or fried parsley and slices or wedges of lemon or lime. The wedges give more juice but are not as delicately decorative as the slices, which might be sprinkled with chopped parsley or paprika.

Garnishes for cold fish are bouquets of fresh parsley or water cress, thinly sliced cucumbers, little plum or cherry tomatoes, chopped egg, or a mayonnaise—either a mayonnaise that is green with chopped herbs (tarragon, chives, and dill, usually)—or a MAYONNAISE of natural creamy yellow.

How to Cook Lobsters or Shrimp in COURT BOUILLON

4 *quarts water* (See note below)	3 *bay leaves*
1 *cup white vinegar*	1 *teaspoon dried thyme*
1 *carrot, sliced*	1 *teaspoon crushed peppercorns*
2 *large onions, sliced*	*Pinch caraway* (optional)
6 *stalks celery, sliced*	3 *tablespoons salt*

Bring all ingredients to a boil and cook for 10 minutes. Add lobsters or shrimp. Bring to a boil again, then reduce heat to a simmer. Cook lobsters 5 minutes for the first pound and 3 minutes for each additional pound. Cook shrimp 5 minutes only. Cool in the Court Bouillon, then remove from liquid and refrigerate until ready to use.

Note: 4 quarts is only sufficient liquid for 3 1½-pound lobsters or 5 pounds of shrimp. To cook 6 or 10 pounds of shrimp, double the amount of water.

BAKED CRABMEAT A L'IMPERIALE

(Serves 4)

2 *tablespoons butter,*
  divided
1 *green pepper, chopped*
  fine
1 *small onion, chopped fine*
1 *teaspoon dry mustard*
1 *teaspoon French mustard*
¼ *cup brandy*

½ *cup fine bread crumbs,*
  divided
¼ *teaspoon salt*
½ *cup* BASIC CREAM
  SAUCE
1 *pound fresh crabmeat*
2 *tablespoons grated*
  Parmesan cheese

Melt 1 tablespoon butter in a large saucepan. Stir in green pepper and onion; simmer about 10 minutes. Remove from heat and add both kinds of mustard, brandy, ¼ cup bread crumbs, salt, and Cream Sauce. Blend thoroughly. Then mix in the crabmeat gently so as not to break up the pieces. Heat for several minutes without too much stirring.

Spoon into a buttered baking dish or 4 individual shells. Sprinkle surface with a mixture of grated cheese and remaining ¼ cup bread crumbs. Dribble on the remaining melted butter and bake in a preheated 450° F (or hot) oven until top is golden brown. Takes about 20 minutes for the baking dish, 12 to 15 minutes for individual shells.

BAKED STUFFED LOBSTER THERMIDOR

(Serves 4)

4 lobsters, 1¼ pounds each
COURT BOUILLON
1 tablespoon butter
6 shallots, chopped fine
1 pound mushrooms, sliced
1 tablespoon dry mustard
½ cup dry white wine
½ teaspoon salt
Dash paprika
Dash cayenne pepper

3 cups thick BASIC CREAM
SAUCE, divided
1 teaspoon dried tarragon
¼ cup cognac
¼ cup heavy cream,
whipped
½ cup HOLLANDAISE SAUCE
2 to 3 tablespoons grated
Parmesan cheese

Cook lobsters in Court Bouillon, allowing them to cool in the liquid. When cool, split down the middle, trim off claws, crack, and remove meat. Remove all meat from lobster body and cut into large dice. Set aside. Wash out lobster shells and place on a baking sheet.

Melt butter in a large saucepan. Stir in shallots and cook several minutes. Add mushrooms and continue cooking 5 minutes longer. Stir frequently. Add lobster meat, mustard, wine, salt, paprika, cayenne pepper and 2 cups thick cream sauce. Return to heat and simmer over a low fire for 10 minutes, stirring occasionally. Remove from heat and blend in tarragon and cognac. Taste and add more salt if necessary.

Spoon mixture into lobster shells. Combine remaining cup of cream sauce with the whipped cream and Hollandaise Sauce. Spread a covering of this topping over the lobster filling, then sprinkle with grated cheese. Bake in a preheated 450° F (or hot) oven for 20 to 25 minutes. If tops are not delicately browned at this point, place under broiler for a minute or two.

CRABMEAT A LA DEWEY

(Serves 6)

2 tablespoons butter
½ pound mushrooms, thinly
   sliced
1 green pepper, cut into
   thin strips
1 slice pimento, cut into
   thin strips
½ cup sherry

2 pounds crabmeat
1 teaspoon salt
Pinch cayenne pepper
3 cups BASIC CREAM
   SAUCE, divided
¼ cup grated Swiss cheese
½ cup grated Parmesan
   cheese, divided

Melt butter in a large saucepan. Stir in mushrooms, green pepper, and pimento; cook over a low heat for about 8 to 10 minutes. Add sherry, crabmeat, salt, and cayenne pepper; toss a minute or so just as you would a salad (take care not to break up the lumps). Blend in 1 cup hot Basic Cream Sauce. Then spoon into individual baking shells or 1 large baking dish.

Reheat remaining 2 cups of Cream Sauce with grated cheese and half the grated Parmesan for a minute or so. Cover crabmeat mixture with this sauce, sprinkle with remaining Parmesan cheese and bake in preheated 500° F (or very hot) oven for about 8 to 10 minutes or until piping hot.

SEAFOOD A LA NEWBURG

(Serves 4 to 5)

2 tablespoons butter
½ pound fresh scallops
½ pound cooked lobster
   meat, cut in chunks
½ pound cooked
   crabmeat
½ pound cooked shrimp,
   cut in half

1 tablespoon paprika
1 teaspoon salt
⅓ cup sherry
2 cups heavy cream
2 tablespoons BASIC CREAM
   SAUCE, divided
4 egg yolks

Melt butter in a saucepan, add the uncooked scallops and simmer 5 minutes. Then add the lobster, crabmeat, and shrimp; sauté for a few minutes. Mix in paprika and salt thoroughly. Add sherry, 1½ cups heavy cream and Cream Sauce. Mix very carefully so as not to break up the fish; bring to a boil slowly. Beat the egg yolks and combine with remaining cream. Add a little of the hot-cream mixture to the egg-cream mixture. Then gradually combine the two mixtures. Bring to a boil again. Take care not to curdle the sauce with overcooking. Taste for seasoning; a dash more salt perhaps.

Serve with RICE PILAF, on toast or in patty shells.

LOBSTER AND SHRIMP CUTLETS LONGCHAMPS

(Serves 6 to 8)

2 cups diced fresh lobster
meat

1 pound fresh shrimp,
diced

3 tablespoons butter,
divided

½ cup flour

1½ cups milk

2 tablespoons brandy

1 teaspoon lemon juice

¼ teaspoon dry mustard

1 teaspoon finely chopped
chives

1 teaspoon salt

¼ teaspoon pepper

3 egg yolks

For Breading:
Flour
2 whole eggs
Dry bread or cracker
crumbs

Chop lobster and shrimp in a coarse dice, measure correct amount and set aside.

Melt 2 tablespoons butter in a saucepan. Stir in flour as well as possible. Pour in milk and cook over a low heat, stirring vigorously, until bubbly. This makes a very thick cream sauce.

Melt remaining tablespoon butter in a skillet, add lobster and shrimp, cook over a low heat for about 5 minutes. Stir in brandy, lemon juice, mustard, chives, salt and pepper. Last of all blend in the thick cream sauce and 3 well-beaten egg yolks. Remove from heat and cool.

Shape the mixture into cutlets or croquettes, dust with flour, dip into well-beaten whole eggs and coat with crumbs. Fry in deep fat, preheated to 375° F, for several minutes until crisp and golden. Drain on paper towels.

CURRIED FRESH SEAFOOD CALCUTTA

(Serves 6 to 8)

Sauce:

6 *tablespoons butter*
1 *large onion, sliced*
1 *leek, sliced*
3 *stalks celery, sliced*
Few sprigs parsley
1 *clove garlic, crushed*
1 *bay leaf*
1 *teaspoon dried thyme*
4 *tablespoons flour*

4 *tablespoons curry powder*
2 *green apples, cored and sliced*
1 *tablespoon tomato purée*
½ *cup shredded coconut*
1 *quart chicken broth* (See note below)
1 *teaspoon salt*
¼ *teaspoon sugar*

Seafood:

6 *tablespoons butter*
1 *cup scallops*
1 *cup cooked lobster*

1 *cup cooked shrimp*
1 *cup cooked crabmeat*
1 *cup light cream*

Melt butter in a large saucepan. Add onion, leek, celery, parsley, garlic, bay leaf, and thyme; cook over a low heat, stirring frequently, until mixture is a golden brown. Stir in flour and curry powder, then add apple slices, tomato purée, coconut, chicken broth, salt, and sugar. Bring to a boil, reduce heat, and simmer over a low heat for 1 hour. Strain. Set the sauce aside until seafood is prepared.

Melt the butter in a saucepan. Add scallops, cover and cook

for 2 to 3 minutes. Stir in lobster, shrimp, crabmeat. Cover and cook 2 to 3 minutes. Now add the curry sauce and cream. Taste and add more curry powder if you like a hotter curry. Serve with pilaf of rice and a good chutney.

Note: Or use 4 chicken bouillon cubes dissolved in 1 quart boiling water.

LONGCHAMPS FRIED PRAWNS OR SHRIMP

(Serves 4 to 6)

2 *pounds large raw shrimp*	*Juice of 1 lemon*
½ *teaspoon salt*	1 *tablespoon chopped*
Pinch of pepper	*parsley or chives*

Peel and devein the raw shrimp, cutting down the back with a sharp knife, just deep enough for the two halves of the shrimp to open and lie flat. Put in a bowl with salt, pepper, lemon juice, chopped parsley or chives. Refrigerate for 2 hours or longer.

French Fritter Batter:

2 *eggs, separated*	½ *cup beer*
½ *cup flour*	1 *tablespoon melted butter*
¼ *teaspoon salt*	

Combine the beaten egg yolks with flour and salt until smooth. Stir in beer and melted butter. Set aside in a warm spot until you are ready to fry the shrimp. At this point beat egg whites until they hold a shape. Fold into yolk mixture thoroughly.

Heat deep fat to 350° F or until a 1-inch cube of bread browns in 60 seconds. Dip shrimp first in flour, then in batter. Drop into fat (not too many at a time) and fry until crisp and golden. Takes about 5 minutes. Drain on paper towels.

Serve hot with TARTAR SAUCE.

BROCHETTE OF SEAFOOD COMBINATION LONGCHAMPS

(Serves 4)

16 *raw shrimp, deveined and split*

1 *pound of sea scallops*

1 *pound of swordfish, cut into 1-inch cubes*

8 *claws or chunks of cooked lobster*

8 *large mushroom caps, sautéed slowly in butter for 10 minutes*

8 *1½-inch squares of green pepper, slightly boiled*

8 *1½-inch squares of pimento*

6 *tablespoons of* MAITRE D'HOTEL BUTTER

Place shrimp, scallops, swordfish, and lobster in a marinade of 1 teaspoon of Worcestershire sauce, the juice of 1 lemon, a few drops of oil, 1 tablespoon of chopped parsley or finely cut chives, and a pinch of salt. Let stand a few hours.

Thread on 4 skewers (8 inches long) alternately as follows: mushroom cap, lobster meat, shrimp (2), green pepper, red pimento, swordfish, and scallops (2). Repeat until skewer is filled. Close with a second mushroom cap. Dust each brochette with paprika, sprinkle with oil. Broil slowly, turning occasionally, for 15 minutes.

Transfer brochette to hot platter or individual plates. Spoon Maitre D'Hotel Butter over the brochettes. As an accompaniment serve French-fried potatoes, crisp and brown, on one side of the skewer and green peas on the other side. Garnish with lemon wedges and bouquet of fresh parsley.

MAITRE D'HOTEL BUTTER

6 *tablespoons of melted
    butter*
1 *tablespoon of chopped
    parsley*
1 *teaspoon of
    Worcestershire sauce*

*Juice of 2 lemons
Salt and pepper to taste
Dash cayenne pepper*

Mix ingredients thoroughly and heat. Do not boil.

SUPREME OF POMPANO A LA MITCHELL

(Serves 6)

6 *filets of pompano*
¾ *cup cognac*
Juice of 1 lemon
½ *cup wild rice*
6 *shallots, finely chopped*
12 *mushroom caps, cut in
    fine sticks*
¼ *cup fish stock or clam
    juice*
½ *cup dry white wine,
    preferably Neuchâtel*

2 *tablespoons flour*
4 *tablespoons butter, divided*
1 *cup heavy cream*
4 *tablespoons* HOLLANDAISE
    SAUCE
2 *tablespoons whipped
    cream, unsweetened*
Salt
2 *large truffles, cut in fine
    sticks* (optional)

Lay pompano in a large shallow container. Pour cognac
and lemon juice over filets and allow to marinate for 30 to
40 minutes.

Cook wild rice in boiling, salted water until tender. At the
end of the marinating period, transfer fish to a buttered shallow pan. Over the top, sprinkle shallots, mushrooms, fish
stock or clam juice, wine, and the cognac-lemon mixture
you used as a marinade. Bring to a boil, then reduce heat and

cook gently for 10 to 12 minutes or until fish is tender when tested with a fork.

Drain rice thoroughly and place in a large, shallow serving dish (one that is ovenproof) and, using a broad spatula, arrange filets with mushrooms on top of rice. Keep warm.

Cook liquid in which fish cooked until it is reduced to a third of the original amount. Blend together flour and 2 tablespoons butter. Stir into fish liquid, add heavy cream and cook, stirring constantly, until sauce bubbles. Remove from heat and stir in remaining 2 tablespoons butter, the Hollandaise Sauce, whipped cream, and enough salt to please your taste.

Sprinkle truffles over the pompano, pour sauce over all and place under a preheated broiler until nicely browned.

SCALLOPS AND MUSHROOMS IN WHITE WINE
SAUCE [*Fettucine Verazzano*]

(Serves 6 to 8)

6 *tablespoons butter,* *divided*	1 *teaspoon salt*
12 *shallots, chopped fine*	Pinch cayenne pepper
2 *pounds scallops*	3 *tablespoons flour*
½ *pound mushrooms,* *sliced thin*	½ *cup light cream*
2 *cups dry white wine*	2 *tablespoons finely sliced* *chives*
Juice of 2 lemons	*Chopped parsley*

Grease a large saucepan lavishly with 2 tablespoons butter. Sprinkle shallots over bottom, then add scallops (if sea scallops are used, cut in quarters), mushrooms, white wine, lemon juice, salt, and cayenne. Bring to a boil, place a piece of buttered waxed paper directly over the mixture, then simmer over a low heat for 10 minutes. Lift scallops and mushrooms from liquid and keep warm. Boil liquid over a brisk heat until it is reduced to half. Add the 4 remaining tablespoons of butter mixed together smoothly with the flour and cook, stirring constantly, until sauce thickens. Stir in cream, boil once more, then remove from heat and stir in scallops, mushrooms, and chives. Serve over hot buttered EGG NOODLES with a sprinkling of chopped parsley.

ABALONE STEAKS IN RHINE WINE SAUCE

(Serves 4)

12 *shallots, finely chopped*	3 *tablespoons lemon juice*
1 *pound abalone steaks*	1 *teaspoon salt*
(See note below)	*Dash cayenne pepper*
½ *cup butter*	1 *tablespoon flour*
½ *pound small whole*	½ *cup heavy cream*
mushrooms	3 *tablespoons chopped chives*
1½ *cups Rhine wine*	

Butter bottom and sides of a saucepan. Sprinkle in the shallots and place abalone steaks on top. Dot with 4 tablespoons butter. Add mushrooms, wine, lemon juice, salt, and cayenne pepper. Bring to a boil, then reduce heat, cover and simmer gently for 10 minutes. Transfer abalone and mushrooms to a plate and keep warm.

Boil liquid in which abalone cooked until reduced in half. Stir in flour mixed together smoothly with remaining butter (this is a *beurre manié*) and cook until sauce is smooth and slightly thick. Add cream and bring to a boil once again. Stir in chives last of all. Serve abalone steaks on a bed of hot noodles and pour the sauce over all.

Note: 1 pound of bay or sea scallops can be used in place of abalone steaks.

BROOK TROUT SAUTE AMANDINE

(Serves 6)

Allow 1 trout per person. Leave whole with head and tail intact. Simply clean and wash.

For 6 trout, dip fish in cold milk; cover lightly with flour; season with salt and pepper. Melt 6 tablespoons butter in a skillet. Add trout and sauté over a gentle heat for about 5 minutes per side. Transfer to a heated platter and keep warm.

Add 2 more tablespoons butter to the same pan and heat until foamy. Stir in 2 tablespoons blanched, shredded almonds and cook for a minute or so, rocking the pan back and forth. Place fish on serving platter, spoon 1 teaspoon lemon juice, a few drops of Worcestershire and some of the golden-brown almond-butter mixture over each fish. Garnish with parsley and lemon wedges.

Serve with little boiled potatoes tossed in chopped chives or parsley.

BROILED BOSTON SCROD MAITRE D'HOTEL

(Serves 6)

3 *large filets of scrod*	1 *cup fresh bread crumbs*
Salt and pepper to taste	½ *cup salad oil*

Cut each filet in half. Sprinkle with salt and pepper. Cover with bread crumbs and place on a well-oiled broiling pan. Moisten the fish with salad oil and broil in a preheated broiler, 4 inches from unit, for 8 to 10 minutes or until scrod is tender when tested with a fork. Garnish scrod with parsley, a wedge of lemon, and serve with potatoes and a vegetable.

Serve hot with MAITRE D'HOTEL BUTTER.

POACHED HALIBUT WITH CREAMY EGG SAUCE

(Serves 4)

1 *cup milk*	*Dash white pepper*
1 *cup light cream*	2 *hard-cooked eggs*
2 *small onions, sliced thin*	4 *halibut steaks, 8 ounces*
Half a bay leaf	*each*
1 *whole clove*	*Juice of 1 lemon*
3 *tablespoons butter*	1 *bay leaf*
3 *tablespoons flour*	1 *tablespoon salt*
1 *teaspoon salt*	

Make the sauce first: Heat milk and cream together with thin slices of onion, bay leaf, and whole clove until film shines on surface. Melt butter in a saucepan. Stir in flour smoothly and cook over a low heat for several minutes. Pour in scalded-milk mixture and cook over a low heat, stirring constantly, until mixture bubbles. Remove from heat, season with salt and white pepper. Strain into a saucepan and stir in coarsely chopped eggs. If sauce is too thick, add more light cream. Keep hot until fish is poached.

Place halibut steaks in a large skillet. Almost cover with cold water. Season with lemon juice, bay leaf, salt. Bring to a boil, then reduce heat and allow to simmer for about 10 minutes or until tender when tested with a fork. Drain thoroughly and serve with the egg sauce.

TROUT WITH WHITE GRAPES [*Truite Véronique*]

(Serves 4)

4 *brook trout*	4 *tablespoons salad oil*
Salt	*Juice of 1 lemon*
Pepper	½ *cup butter*
2 *tablespoons milk*	1 *can (8¾ ounces)*
2 *tablespoons flour*	*seedless grapes, drained*

Have the trout split from the inside and all bones removed (it's practical to have your fish man do this). Head
and tail should remain intact. Sprinkle fish with salt and pepper, brush with milk, and coat with flour.

Heat oil in a large skillet, add trout, and sauté over a moderate heat until golden brown on both sides. This takes approximately 3 minutes per side. Be sure to turn trout carefully with a broad spatula. Place on a warm serving platter,
sprinkle with lemon juice, and keep warm.

Discard all fat in skillet, add butter, and heat until lightly
browned and foamy. Add the drained grapes, then spoon over
the trout.

Garnish platter with lemon wedges, parsley, broiled tomatoes and small boiled potatoes.

POACHED SALMON STEAKS AU COURT BOUILLON

(Serves 6)

6 *salmon steaks*, 8 *to* 10 *ounces each*
2 *quarts* COURT BOUILLON

For the Court Bouillon—bring to a boil and cook for 10
minutes:

2 *quarts water*	*Few ribs celery, sliced*
1 *cup white wine or* ½ *cup*	1 *bay leaf*
white vinegar	6 *crushed peppercorns*
1 *small carrot, sliced thin*	4 *cloves*
1 *onion, sliced thin*	1½ *teaspoons salt*
Few sprigs parsley	

Arrange the salmon steaks, side by side, in a pan large
enough to accommodate them without crowding. Strain the
Court Bouillon over the fish, using just enough to cover. Bring
to a slow boil; lower the heat and let simmer from 8 to 10

minutes. Remove from the heat and let stand few minutes more.

Remove salmon steaks from the Court Bouillon carefully, using a large spatula or flat skimmer. Place on covered hot platter. Garnish with lemon quarters and bouquet of fresh parsley.

Serve with HOLLANDAISE SAUCE and plain boiled potatoes. If the steaks are served cold the Hollandaise Sauce can be replaced, if desired, with MAYONNAISE, REMOULADE or TARTAR SAUCE or GREEN MAYONNAISE.

FILETS OF SOLE MARGUERY

(Serves 6)

12 *small filets of sole, plus bones from the sole*	½ *teaspoon salt*
	Dash pepper
1 *bay leaf*	12 *large mushrooms, sliced thin*
1 *small onion, sliced*	
1 *carrot, sliced*	12 *large cooked shrimp*
4 *stalks celery, sliced*	12 *oysters*
½ *cup butter*	*Juice of 2 lemons*
3 *tablespoons flour*	1 *cup dry white wine*
2 *tablespoons chopped shallots*	½ *cup heavy cream, whipped*

Set filets of sole aside while you make the fish stock. Combine fish bones, bay leaf, onion, carrot, celery, and 1 quart of water in a saucepan. Cover and cook over a moderate heat for 20 minutes. Strain. Reserve the liquid.

Melt butter in a saucepan. Stir in flour smoothly and cook a minute or two. Add 2 cups of the fish stock and cook, stirring constantly, until sauce bubbles. Reduce heat and simmer slowly for about 15 minutes longer. Set aside.

Butter a large shallow pan generously. In the bottom sprinkle the shallots, salt, and pepper. Fold each filet of sole in half and place them side by side on top of the shallots. Pile mushrooms, shrimp, and oysters on the filets. Add lemon juice, white wine, any remaining fish stock, a little more salt and pepper. Put a sheet of buttered waxed paper on top and cover with a lid. Cook over a low heat for 10 to 12 minutes or until sole is tender when tested with a fork. Transfer filets, mushrooms, shrimp, and oysters to a large platter and keep warm. Cook liquid in which fish poached over a high heat until it has cooked down to several tablespoons, then stir it into the thickened fish sauce. Stir in the whipped cream and pour over the fish. Place in a preheated broiler, about 4 inches from broiling unit, for several minutes or until surface is a delicate gold. Serve with boiled potatoes.

SUPREME OF ENGLISH SOLE A LA JOAN SUTHERLAND

(Serves 6)

Filets of 6 English sole
(about 2¼ pounds)
¼ cup cognac
Juice of 1 lemon
6 shallots, finely chopped
12 mushrooms, sliced thin
¼ cup fish stock (See
note below)
½ cup dry white wine,
preferably Neuchâtel
1 cup uncooked wild rice,
approximately 2 cups
cooked

2 tablespoons flour
4 tablespoons butter
½ cup heavy cream
2 tablespoons unsweetened
whipped cream
4 tablespoons HOLLANDAISE
SAUCE
4 tablespoons butter

Place filets of sole in large, flat dish. Add cognac and lemon juice. Marinate for at least half an hour, spooning marinade over the fish occasionally. Butter a saucepan large enough to hold the filets comfortably. Add fish, the marinade, shallots, mushrooms, fish stock, and wine. Bring to a boil. Turn heat down to simmer; cover and poach for 10 to 12 minutes or until fish flakes easily when pierced with a fork. Make a bed of the hot wild rice on a flameproof platter, place the filets on top and scatter mushrooms over all.

Reduce liquid in pan over high heat to about one third. Work 2 tablespoons flour into 4 tablespoons of butter to make a *beurre manié*. Add, bit by bit, to broth, stirring constantly, until smooth. Then add heavy cream and boil for a few minutes. Take pan off the stove and stir in whipped cream, Hollandaise Sauce and remaining butter. Pour sauce over fish and wild rice. Place in a preheated 375° F oven until bubbly and delicately brown on top.

Note: Bottled clam juice can be substituted for fish stock.

FILET OF SOLE CAPRICE

(Serves 4)

4 *filets of sole, about* 1½ *pounds*	¼ *pound butter, divided*
Salt	*Juice of* ½ *lemon*
Pepper	2 *bananas*
Flour	*Sugar*
2 *eggs, well beaten*	¼ *cup slivered almonds* (See note below)

Season filets with salt and pepper, dust with flour and dip in eggs. Sauté in 6 tablespoons heated butter, over a moderate heat, until golden brown on each side—takes about 4 minutes per side. When cooked, pour over lemon juice.

Cut bananas in half lengthwise, place on pan cut-side down, sprinkle with a light coating of sugar and place in a preheated broiler for several minutes or until shiny and brown on top.

Melt remaining 2 tablespoons butter in a small saucepan. Toss in almonds and sauté until golden.

Serve fish on a heated platter with a half banana on each filet. Pour almonds and butter over all and garnish with lemon wedges and parsley.

Note: You can use canned almonds, slivered and toasted.

Poultry

"A chicken in every pot!" Henry IV was the first to put this thought into words. It was his promise of prosperity for France. And since then, of course, it has become a familiar campaign promise.

It is never a turkey, goose, duckling, or other bird that is promised. Understandably, it is a chicken. Other birds are splendid. But a chicken is a most practical and accommodating bird. It is not by chance that the chapter that follows offers many chicken recipes for each one for turkey or duck.

Chicken may be boiled, broiled, roasted, or fried. It takes to rice and to noodles. It yields its flavor to such herbs as tarragon, saffron, and thyme. It marries blissfully with wine, with curry, with tomatoes. It provides a subtle contrast in taste when it is baked with vegetables under the rich and flaky crust of a pie. Its leftovers, should there be any, can be chopped into a creamed-chicken hash which, topped with a poached egg, provides a delicious luncheon or a gala Sunday breakfast. Or it can be turned into what probably is the most perennially popular salad or layered into a CLUB SANDWICH, which it has, it would appear, invested with a kind of immortality. Or, perched on a slice of ham, aided and abetted with a tarragon leaf or two, it can be blanketed with a glistening aspic. And its carcass, like that of the turkey's or the duck's, provides a tasty soup.

A turkey, if it is a young bird, can be broiled. But turkey, usually, looks to its stuffing for its versatility: oyster, CHESTNUT, SAUSAGE MEAT, wild rice with pine or pistachio nuts, or good old-fashioned bread and onion, and sage or thyme.

Ducks, geese, pheasants, guinea and Cornish hens, too, tend to find their greatest versatility through their dressings.

Whichever bird is selected and whatever its preparation is to be it is essential the bird be tasty and tender. Poultry dishes, like every other item of food, cannot be any better than what goes into them.

When I shop for Longchamps poultry I look for birds with smooth white skin with the faintest tinge of blue, with soft feet, with a flexible breastbone and the cartilage at its tip tender.

The "dressed weight" of a plucked bird includes the weight of the head, feet, and organs.

Hens, of course, provide the plumpest breasts.

Broilers, from 2 to 4 months old, weigh from 1½ to 2½ pounds.

Roasters, from 4 to 8 months old, weigh 3 to 4 pounds.

Capons, which are castrated male birds, weigh more.

Pullets, which are hens, weigh less.

Fowls, a year and older, incline to be tough. But cooked long and slowly they fortify soups and fricassees with rich flavor.

In the Longchamps kitchens, when chicken in parts is broiled, boiled, or roasted, we allow from five to ten minutes more for second joints and drumsticks than for breasts. White meat cooks faster.

And always we carve turkey as it is served. The meat of this bird dries out rapidly.

BREAST OF CHICKEN SAUTE EUGENIE

(Serves 4)

4 breasts of chicken	12 fresh mushroom caps
Salt and pepper to taste	4 slices of toast, trimmed
4 tablespoons of butter	4 slices smoked ham

For Sauce:

2 tablespoons of flour	1 teaspoon paprika
¼ cup sherry wine	1 cup light cream

Season chicken breasts with salt and pepper. Heat butter in large frying pan and when it foams place chicken breasts in it. Cover and cook over medium heat for about 15 to 20 minutes, or until golden brown, turning each breast once and shaking the pan occasionally. Five minutes before the chickens are cooked add the mushroom caps. Remove pan from fire, take out chicken and mushrooms. To the butter that remains in the pan add the flour and blend well. Then add sherry wine, paprika, and light cream, scalded. Stir continuously until sauce thickens. Return to the heat and bring to a boil. Place the chicken and mushrooms in the sauce and let all cook together from 8 to 10 minutes.

On a deep serving platter arrange the trimmed and hot toast, side by side. Lay a slice of heated ham on each slice of toast, then a chicken breast and then the mushrooms, 3 caps to each. Adjust the sauce to your taste and laddle it evenly over the chicken. With it serve, separately, rice, EGG NOODLES, asparagus tips, peas, or string beans.

CHICKEN SAUTE A LA PROVENCALE

(Serves 2)

1 2-pound chicken, cut in quarters	Few sprigs celery leaves
1 teaspoon salt	Few sprigs parsley
¼ teaspoon pepper	1 bay leaf
2 tablespoons olive oil	½ cup dry white wine
1 tablespoon butter	4 ripe tomatoes, peeled, seeded; pulp cut fine
4 small white onions	1 teaspoon arrowroot
½ pound mushrooms, quartered if large	12 large black olives, cut from pit
2 cloves garlic, unpeeled	Parsley

Season chicken with salt and pepper. Sauté in a mixture of heated oil and butter until golden on both sides. Add the onions, mushrooms, and garlic, along with celery leaves, parsley, and bay leaf tied together in a little bouquet. Cook slowly for a few minutes, pour in wine; cover, and cook a few more minutes to reduce the liquid. Now add tomatoes; cover again, and cook until chicken is tender. Total cooking time for chicken is approximately 40 minutes.

Transfer chicken to a deep serving dish and keep warm. Remove and discard seasoning bouquet and garlic.

Combine arrowroot smoothly with a little white wine and stir into tomato mixture along with black olives; cook, stirring constantly, until sauce boils. Taste to see if more salt is needed. Pour over chicken and sprinkle with chopped parsley. Serve with RICE PILAF.

CHICKEN IN BROTH WITH DUMPLINGS
[*Pot au Feu Henry IV*]

(Serves 4)

TO PREPARE CHICKENS:

2 2½-pound chickens, quartered	Few sprigs parsley
	1 bay leaf
2 medium onions, quartered	4 cloves
2 carrots, cut in chunks	1 clove garlic
2 leeks, split lengthwise	1 teaspoon salt
1 stalk celery	

Place quartered chickens in a large kettle, pour in enough water to almost cover and season with onions, carrots, leeks, celery, parsley, bay leaf, cloves, garlic, and salt. Bring to a boil; cover, reduce heat and simmer gently until chicken is very tender when tested with a fork. Takes 35 to 40 minutes. Transfer chickens to a bowl and set aside.

Place kettle with broth back over high heat and boil hard until there is approximately 1½ quarts of liquid left. Strain, skim off all chicken fat, and reserve to use later on.

TO PREPARE SOUP:

¼ cup chicken fat
¼ cup flour
1½ quarts chicken broth
Salt
Pinch white pepper
½ pound mushrooms,
    sliced
1 tablespoon butter

2 tablespoons cooked green
    peas
2 tablespoons cooked green
    beans, Frenched
1 tablespoon chopped chives
MARROW DUMPLINGS or
    MATZOH BALLS

Heat ¼ cup chicken fat in a saucepan. Stir in flour smoothly and cook a minute or so. Pour in chicken broth, season with salt and pepper. Cook, stirring constantly, until bubbly and thick as heavy cream. Simmer gently about 30 minutes. Then add mushrooms, sautéed in heated butter for 5 minutes, peas, green beans, and Marrow Dumplings or Matzoh Balls. Cook about 5 minutes longer. Remove and discard skin and breast bones from chickens and place 2 quarters in each soup plate. Cover with the hot soup and sprinkle with chives.

BREAST OF CHICKEN MARYLAND

(Serves 4)

4 chicken breasts
Salt
Pepper
Flour
2 eggs, well beaten
1 cup fine dry bread crumbs

4 tablespoons butter
1 cup BASIC CREAM SAUCE
4 CORN FRITTERS
POTATO CROQUETTES
Bacon strips

Remove breast bones from chicken or ask your butcher to do it for you. Season chicken with salt and pepper, coat lightly with flour, dip in eggs. Cover evenly with crumbs. Sauté in heated butter over a low heat until golden brown on both sides. Takes 15 to 20 minutes. Pour hot Cream Sauce on heated serving platter. Arrange chicken breasts on top of sauce and garnish with Corn Fritters, Potato Croquettes, and strips of crisp bacon.

CHICKEN CHOW MEIN

(Serves 4)

4 breasts of chicken
4 tablespoons butter
1 cup shredded celery
½ cup shredded onions
½ cup button mushrooms
½ cup bamboo shoots
½ cup shredded bok choy
½ cup water chestnuts, sliced
1 teaspoon monosodium glutamate

Pinch of: salt, pepper, sugar
1 cup bean sprouts
½ cup chicken broth or water
1 tablespoon cornstarch
1 cup fried Chinese noodles
½ cup roasted almonds

Remove skin and bones from chicken and cut in long slim strips (julienne). Heat butter in skillet. Sauté chicken for a few minutes, then add celery, onions, mushrooms, bamboo shoots, bok choy, and chestnuts. Season with monosodium glutamate, salt, pepper, and sugar. Sauté for a few minutes. Add bean sprouts. Mix chicken broth with cornstarch and add this mixture, slowly, to the vegetables and chicken. Stir constantly. Let cook 5 minutes. Then remove from heat. Serve in chafing dish or casserole. Top with fried Chinese noodles and roasted almonds.

CHICKEN SAUTE IN RED WINE [Coq au Vin Rouge]
(Serves 8)

2 chickens, 2½ to 3
    pounds, quartered
3 cups dry red wine
2 medium onions, chopped
2 stalks celery, chopped
2 cloves garlic, crushed
2 bay leaves
½ teaspoon dried thyme
Salt

Pepper
3 tablespoons butter
½ cup cognac
2 cans (7½-ounce size)
    beef gravy
12 small white onions,
6 strips bacon
1 pound small mushrooms
Chopped parsley

Place quartered chickens in a shallow dish or pan, pour a mixture of red wine, onions, celery, garlic, bay leaves, and thyme over all; refrigerate overnight, turning the chicken pieces as convenient.

The following day lift chicken from marinade and pat dry with paper towels. Sprinkle with salt and pepper, then sauté in heated butter until golden brown on each side. Stir in vegetables from marinade and cook several minutes. Heat cognac, ignite with a match, and pour over chicken. When flames die out, add wine from marinade and the beef gravy. Bring to a boil, cover, and cook over a low heat for about 30 minutes or until chicken is tender. Transfer chicken to serving casserole. Strain the sauce (discard vegetables) and set aside.

Cook onions in a little boiling salted water until tender. Drain. Cut bacon into thin strips and fry until almost crisp. Remove bacon from fat and toss in mushrooms and cooked onions. Cook, stirring frequently, for about 5 minutes.

Add whole mushrooms, onions, and bacon to strained sauce. Taste for seasoning. Pour over chicken and sprinkle with chopped parsley. Serve with buttered EGG NOODLES, RICE PILAF, or mashed potatoes.

CHICKEN A LA KING

(Serves 6)

4 tablespoons butter	Dash cayenne
1 cup mushroom slices	4 egg yolks
1 green pepper, sliced thin	½ cup cream
½ cup dry sherry	3 cups sliced boiled chicken
2 cups BASIC CREAM SAUCE	1 tablespoon pimento, sliced
1 teaspoon salt	

Heat butter in a saucepan, add mushrooms and sauté until lightly browned. Stir in green pepper and simmer a few more minutes. Now add sherry, Basic Cream Sauce, salt, and cayenne. Bring to a boil, stirring constantly.

Combine egg yolks with cream. Stir into mushroom mixture along with chicken. Heat through but don't boil. Just before serving, stir in the pimento. Serve on toast, rice, or in patty shells.

BOILED FOWL WITH RICE

(Serves 5 to 6)

1 fowl, 5 to 6 pounds	1 medium onion, chopped
2 tablespoons salt	3 tablespoons butter
1 onion stuck with 3 cloves	2 tablespoons flour
Few celery leaves	2 cups chicken broth
1 bay leaf	½ cup cream
Few sprigs parsley	

Leave fowl whole, trussing wings and legs close to the body. Place in a large kettle and cover with cold water. Add salt, onion stuck with cloves, celery leaves, bay leaf, and parsley; cook to a boil. Reduce heat, cover, and simmer over a low heat for 1½ to 2 hours or until tender. Transfer fowl to a platter and keep warm. Strain the broth.

To make the sauce, cook chopped onion in melted butter for several minutes. Stir in flour as smoothly as possible and cook for a few minutes longer. Do not brown. Pour in 2 cups chicken broth; cook, stirring constantly, until slightly thick. Add cream and continue cooking several minutes longer. Taste and add more salt, if necessary.

To serve, make a bed of steamed rice on a serving platter. Carve the fowl and arrange on top of the rice. Pour half the sauce over chicken and rice. Serve remainder on the side.

EMINCE OF CHICKEN MEXICAINE
(Serves 4 to 6)

1 fowl, 4 to 5 pounds	¼ cup white wine
Salt and pepper	2 cans (8-ounce size)
1 tablespoon olive oil	tomato sauce
½ pound mushrooms,	1 teaspoon salt
sliced thin	¼ teaspoon pepper
2 green peppers, cut in	Dash Tabasco
thin strips	

Quarter the fowl and put into a kettle with enough water to almost cover. Season with salt and pepper, cover and bring to a boil. Reduce heat and simmer over a low heat for 1½ to 2 hours or until tender. Let cool in the chicken stock. When cool enough to handle comfortably, remove skin and strip meat from bones in large pieces. Set aside.

Heat olive oil in a saucepan. Add mushrooms and green peppers. Cook over a low heat, stirring occasionally, for 10 minutes. Pour in wine and cook 10 minutes longer or until liquid is reduced. Add tomato sauce, bring to a boil, and season with salt, pepper, and Tabasco. Add chicken pieces to sauce and heat a few more minutes. Good with steamed rice, EGG NOODLES or mashed potatoes.

Note: Recipe can be doubled successfully.

DUCKLING A L'ORANGE BIGARADE

(Serves 4)

1 *duck, 5 to 6 pounds*	1 *carrot, coarsely chopped*
Salt and pepper	3 *celery leaves, coarsely*
2 *tablespoons shortening or*	*chopped*
salad oil	1 *bay leaf, crumbled*
1 *onion, coarsely chopped*	½ *teaspoon dried thyme*

Remove any lumps of fat from tail of duck, then truss, tying wings and legs securely. Rub surface with salt and pepper.

Place duck in a fairly large roasting pan, add shortening or oil, and roast in a preheated 500° F, or very hot, oven for 15 to 20 minutes, basting frequently. Turn duck once or twice so it won't stick to bottom of pan. Add onion, carrot, celery leaves, bay leaf, and thyme. Lower heat to 400° F, or moderately hot, and continue roasting for 1½ hours or until tender. You can determine when it is properly cooked if the legs move easily. Keep warm.

Orange Sauce Bigarade:

4 *large oranges*	2 *tablespoons currant jelly*
½ *cup dry white wine*	⅓ *cup Cointreau or Grand*
1 *cup (7½-ounce can)*	*Marnier*
brown gravy	*Dash of salt*
1 *tablespoon sugar*	

While duck is roasting, shred outer rind of oranges (a potato peeler works fine), then julienne the rind by cutting it into thin strips. Parboil the peel in boiling water for a few minutes. Drain. Next, cut off all the white membrane from the oranges and section them. Do this over a bowl to save the juice. Set aside. Add the white wine and gravy to roasting pan, stirring until it is smooth, and simmer for about 15 minutes. Strain into a saucepan.

To finish the sauce, combine the sugar with enough water to moisten (a few drops) and stir over a low heat until golden brown. Add the shredded orange peel, orange juice, currant jelly, Cointreau or Grand Marnier, and cook until jelly has dissolved. Combine with sauce in saucepan, bring to a boil, and simmer about 10 minutes. Skim off all fat that rises to the surface (this may be considerable because of the nature of duck and can be best achieved by using a baster). If sauce seems on the thin side, mix 1 tablespoon cornstarch with 1 tablespoon of the liqueur and stir into sauce. Cook until it has thickened sufficiently. Add salt to taste.

To serve, carve duck and arrange attractively on hot serving platter, spoon half the gravy over the duck, and garnish with orange sections.

Serve remaining sauce in a warm sauceboat.

ROAST TURKEY WITH CHESTNUT-SAUSAGE STUFFING

(Serves 15 to 20)

2 pounds chestnuts
2 tablespoons butter
2 onions, finely chopped
1½ pounds sausage meat
4 to 5 tablespoons milk
1 cup dry bread crumbs
½ teaspoon dried thyme
5 or 6 sprigs parsley, chopped fine
¼ cup cognac
2 whole eggs, slightly beaten
Salt and pepper
1 turkey, 15 to 18 pounds

Cut gashes in the flat side of each chestnut and roast or boil until tender. Remove shells and inner skins. Cool and chop coarsely. This is a bit of a chore, so let us suggest you simplify it all by buying the chestnuts (marrons) imported from France (2 cans, 315 grams each). You simply drain these thoroughly and chop coarsely.

Melt butter in a large skillet, add onions, and cook slowly 4 to 5 minutes. Add sausage meat, breaking it up with a fork. Cook until meat has browned lightly. Stir occasionally. Take off the stove. Mix milk into bread crumbs and add to sausage mixture. Then add thyme, parsley, cognac, eggs, salt and pepper. Finally add the chestnuts and mix thoroughly. Stuff the turkey with this chestnut-sausage mixture. Then truss securely. Rub the bird generously with softened butter and sprinkle with salt and pepper. Roast in a preheated 350° F (or moderate) oven, allowing 18 to 20 minutes per pound. Baste occasionally. You may find you have to add more butter during the roasting period for basting purposes. At the end of the first 2 hours, add the following to the roasting pan:

2 *onions, chopped coarsely*	1 *bay leaf, crushed*
2 *carrots, chopped coarsely*	1 *teaspoon dried thyme*
Few celery leaves, chopped	4 *cloves garlic (whole)*
coarsely	12 *peppercorns, crushed*

Continue roasting the turkey, approximately another 2 hours or until tender. You can determine doneness by squeezing the leg. It is soft and pliable when the bird is properly roasted.

To make gravy:

4 *cups chicken broth or water (preferably broth)*
Salt and pepper
1 *tablespoon cornstarch*

Drain roasting pan of fat. Place pan over high heat. Add chicken broth and stir to loosen all the brown particles that cling to the pan. Cook for ten minutes. Strain into a saucepan, skim off all fat that rises to the surface (a baster is ideal here) add salt and pepper to taste. Mix cornstarch with about a tablespoon of water, stir this into gravy and cook until gravy bubbles and thickens to the degree you like it. Serve in a warm sauceboat.

Note: For a smaller turkey, 9 to 10 pounds, dressed, cut all ingredients in half and roast turkey, at the same temperature, for about 3 hours or 18 to 20 minutes per pound.

Meat

In *Julius Caesar,* you will recall, Shakespeare has the rabble-rousing Cassius ask "Upon what meat doth this our Caesar feed, That he is grown so great?"

For centuries meat has been respected for its energy-giving protein.

About one fourth of our national food budget is spent on meat. It is, therefore, reassuring to know that the cheaper cuts, which take longer to cook and to prepare for cookery, are just as nutritious as the expensive cuts. A *good* lesser cut, like rump or chuck, is, of course, preferable to *an inferior* luxury cut like a rib roast or porterhouse.

Beef is the most nutritious meat of all. Which causes me to wonder if it is man's instinct or his taste buds that makes beef such an overwhelming favorite.

Good beef is bright red in color, marbled with threadlike fat streaks, and open-grained. Its fat is firm and white or creamy. Its suet is crumbly.

Dark-red meat and yellow fat indicate an older animal.

Beef that is to be broiled or roasted will, if hung for a week or two or three, be juicier and tenderer and have a finer flavor.

In the Longchamps kitchens we make it a firm rule that beef, even more importantly than other meats, be removed from the refrigerator in ample time to reach room temperature before it is exposed to the heat.

Corned beef is most succulent when cut from the brisket, soaked from six to ten hours with about three changes of water, and cooked so slowly that it barely simmers, never boils.

Veal, which is very young beef that comes from calves 2½ to 3 months old, is at its best when the animal has fed only on milk or milk and eggs. Milk-fed veal is white with the faintest tinge of pink. The fat is white, smooth as satin, and has a fresh-milk smell.

Usually when calves reach 12 weeks of age they are put out to graze. When there is a faint reddish color to the meat it indicates the animal has had solid food.

Lamb is the English word for the Latin *agnoscere*, which means an ability to recognize a mother from the time of birth. On French menus lamb is *agneau;* which comes closer to the original name.

The term spring lamb does not denote meat that is available only in the spring. It means a young, milk-fed animal not more than five months old. However, since lambs are, largely, born in early spring, this delicacy is more prevalent —and cheaper—from around Easter into early summer.

Lamb, as fresh as lamb should be—which is very fresh indeed—has firm and pinkish meat and fat that is solid, flaky, and white-grained. The younger a lamb the thinner its white, skinlike coating tends to be. This coating, incidentally, should not be removed; it holds in the juices during cooking.

Lamb, rich in protein and easily digested, gives quick energy. I find it strange that it is not a more popular meat nationwide.

Mutton comes from sheep 1½ to 2 years old. It is less tender than lamb and has a richer and heavier flavor. Mutton, roasted, broiled and stewed, is especially popular in England. And mutton chops, in England and here, always have been a chophouse specialty. With mutton, as with lamb, a whiteness of fat suggests freshness.

Ham, the smoked leg or shoulder of a pig, is such a popular food that many countries, even many regions, give it their name; like England's York or Smithfield ham, Czechoslovakia's Prague ham, and our own Virginia ham.

In preparing a country ham the best results will be enjoyed if the accompanying directions are followed faithfully, neither ignored nor modified as being too much trouble.

Pork, the most difficult meat to digest, should be cooked until there is no trace of pink in it.

Pork is also a difficult meat to select. It should be white with, perhaps, a grayish tinge to it, firm and finely grained. Its marbling is so slight that it can be difficult to detect. Its fat should be white and firm. And the less fat that

is visible the better, for there is certain to be fat in the meat itself.

As a pig gets older—and less tender—the meat has a darker tinge, is more pink than gray, and more coarsely grained.

A reliable butcher, who knows his trade—there are many butchers who do not—is a decided asset. He knows when different meats are at their best, most plentiful, and least expensive. He can suggest good substitute cuts. And he can add immeasurably to the appearance of any meat as well as simplify its preparation. He can, for instance, select two chickens of the same weight so they will be ready at precisely the same time. He can, judiciously, trim beef for stew and cut it into small and uniform cubes. He can bone and roll loin chops into delectable *noisettes*.

Never underestimate the friendship of a good butcher.

And, please, never underestimate the need for the recipes that follow to be followed faithfully, particularly where timing is concerned. In meat cookery timing is, almost always, of prime importance.

BEEF STEW IN RED WINE
BOURGUIGNONNE

(Serves 6)

3 *pounds beef*   Few celery leaves
3 *tablespoons shortening*   Few sprigs parsley
3 *tablespoons flour*   2 bay leaves
1½ *teaspoons salt*   ½ pound salt pork, diced
¼ *teaspoon pepper*   24 small white onions
Pinch thyme   1 pound small mushrooms
3 *cloves garlic, crushed*   3 tablespoons butter
4 *cups red wine*   Chopped parsley
1 *cup water*

Cut beef into 2-inch cubes and brown in heated shortening. Sprinkle in the flour and cook, tossing the mixture about, until flour browns. Stir in salt, pepper, thyme, garlic, wine, and water. Bring to a boil; add celery leaves, parsley, and bay leaves. Cover tightly and bake in a preheated 350° F (or moderate) oven for 1½ hours or until tender. Skim off excess fat and discard celery, parsley, and bay leaves.

Brown salt pork in a skillet. When almost crisp add the onions and sauté until lightly browned. Combine salt pork and onions with beef and simmer over direct heat until onions are tender.

Sauté mushrooms in heated butter for 7 to 8 minutes and arrange on top of the beef. Just before serving sprinkle chopped parsley over all.

FILET OF BEEF STROGANOFF

(Serves 4 to 6)

4 tablespoons butter	1 pint sour cream
2 large onions, minced very fine	2 pounds filet of beef, trimmed and sliced thin
½ pound fresh mushrooms, sliced thin	Salt
1 tablespoon paprika	Pepper
1 tablespoon tomato paste	6 tablespoons butter
	Juice of ½ lemon

Melt butter in a large, heavy skillet, add minced onions and cook about 8 minutes. Do not brown. Then add mushrooms, cover, and cook over a low heat for 8 to 10 minutes. Sprinkle on the paprika and simmer, altogether, for a few minutes. Stir in tomato paste. Stir sour cream in thoroughly and set aside.

Keep warm.

Season beef slices with salt and pepper. Melt 6 tablespoons butter in a large frying pan. When very hot, add the meat and cook very quickly over a high heat for 4 to 5 minutes. Add meat to sauce, taste for seasoning, and just before serving, stir in lemon juice. Arrange on a hot platter with a garnish of parsley.

Serve with rice, EGG NOODLES, or mashed potatoes.

MIGNONS OF BEEF TENDERLOIN, LICIA ALBANESE

(Serves 4)

2 *cups* BEARNAISE SAUCE
1½ *pounds fresh*
  mushrooms
1 *tablespoon butter*
2 *tablespoons chopped*
  shallots
Salt
Pepper
1 *tablespoon chopped*
  parsley
2 *tablespoons chopped*
  chives, fresh or frozen

3 *tablespoons* BASIC CREAM
  SAUCE
8 *cooked artichoke hearts,*
  fresh or canned or frozen
2 *tablespoons butter*
8 *small filet mignon*
  (*about ½ inch thick*)
Salt and pepper
6 *tablespoons butter*
8 *large cooked mushroom*
  caps

Prepare the Béarnaise Sauce and keep warm.

Wash mushrooms, dry thoroughly and mince very fine. Melt 1 tablespoon butter in saucepan, add chopped shallots, and cook for about 2 minutes over high heat, stirring constantly. Add minced mushrooms and cook, stirring frequently, until any liquid has been absorbed. Season with salt and pepper to taste. Add chopped parsley, chives, and Basic Cream Sauce. Blend in well and cook a few minutes longer. This makes a very thick paste. Keep warm. Sauté artichoke hearts in 2 tablespoons melted butter over a quick fire until touched with gold. Fill the cavity of each artichoke heart with the mushroom mixture. Keep warm.

Season filets of beef with salt and pepper and sauté over a high heat in 6 tablespoons melted butter for about 2 minutes on each side. Do not overcook. Filets should be rare.

Place one filet on top of each stuffed artichoke, place on a flameproof platter, top with one large cooked mushroom and spoon Béarnaise Sauce over all.

Place in a preheated broiler, 4 inches from tip of flame, and glaze until golden brown. This takes only a few minutes.

Serve immediately with PARISIENNE POTATOES.

HUNGARIAN BEEF GOULASH

(Serves 6)

3 *tablespoons shortening*

3 *cups thinly sliced onions*

2 *cloves garlic, chopped fine*

1 *teaspoon dried marjoram*

3 *pounds lean beef, cut into 1½-inch cubes*

1 *teaspoon salt*

3 *tablespoons paprika*

2 *tablespoons tomato paste*

2 *cups beef broth or water*

Bouquet garni: 4 *sprigs celery leaves,* 4 *sprigs parsley,* 2 *bay leaves*

Heat shortening in a saucepan. Stir in onions and cook over a low heat until straw-colored. Add garlic and marjoram and continue cooking several minutes longer. Toss in cubes of beef, salt, and paprika; mix well. Cover and simmer slowly for 30 minutes, stirring frequently.

Stir in tomato paste, broth or water, and *bouquet garni.* Bring to a boil, reduce heat, cover again, and cook slowly until beef is tender when pierced with a fork—takes about 1 hour. Lift *bouquet garni* out of pan, and discard, skim off any excess fat. Serve with hot EGG NOODLES, SPAETZLES or rice.

BOILED BEEF A LA VIENNA
(Serves 6 to 8)

6 *pounds prime cross rib or short ribs*	6 *leeks, split in half, thoroughly washed*
3 *pounds beef bones, cracked*	4 *carrots*
	2 *onions, stuck with 4 cloves*
1 *gallon water*	*Few sprigs parsley*
3 *teaspoons salt*	2 *bay leaves*
2 *large stalks celery*	12 *peppercorns*

Place the meat and bones in a large soup kettle, add the cold water, and bring to a boil very slowly. As scum rises to the surface, skim it off. When liquid reaches a boil, add all other ingredients, bring to a boil again, then reduce heat and simmer for 2 to 2½ hours or until beef is tender when pierced with a fork.

When cooked, lift meat out of the broth, pull out the bones, trim off any fat, cut into thick slices and place in a deep serving casserole. Strain the broth and skim off all the fat possible (there will be considerable fat, so if you have time, chill the broth in the refrigerator which will bring all the fat to the surface and make it easy to remove).

Pour the strained broth into a saucepan and boil down to about half to make a rich, flavorful concentrate. Taste for seasoning, then pour over meat in casserole.

Serve with boiled potatoes, cooked carrots and, if you like, string beans—making an attractive arrangement in the casserole.

Just before serving, sprinkle generously with finely chopped chives and serve with HORSE-RADISH SAUCE on the side:

3 *tablespoons butter*	3 *tablespoons freshly grated horse-radish or 5 tablespoons prepared*
2 *tablespoons flour*	
2 *cups beef broth*	
¼ *cup fresh white bread crumbs*	*Salt and pepper*
	Dash of sugar

Melt the butter in a saucepan, stir in the flour until smooth. Cook, stirring constantly, a few minutes over low heat. Do not brown. Stir in the beef broth, bring to a boil and cook about 20 minutes, giving it an occasional stir. Take off the heat, stir in bread crumbs, horse-radish, salt, pepper, and sugar. If you use prepared horse-radish, better taste the sauce before adding salt and pepper.

This delicious recipe can be made ahead of time and heated up (the day before, if you like) at the last moment. If you follow this plan, the vegetables should be cooked just in time to add to the casserole.

LONDON BROIL [*Sliced Beefsteak on Toast*]

(Serves 4)

1 *flank steak, about* 2 *pounds* OR	*Salt and pepper to taste*
2 *sirloin steaks,* 1 *pound each*	2 *tablespoons of oil*
	4 *slices toast*
	Melted HERB BUTTER

Sprinkle the steak with salt and pepper. Brush with oil and place on preheated broiler rack about 2 inches from the heat. Broil approximately 5 minutes on each side to desired doneness. Cut diagonally in very thin slices. Arrange on freshly made toast and serve with hot Herb Butter poured over the steak.

Herb Butter:

4 *tablespoons of butter*	1 *teaspoon of*
Juice of 1 *lemon*	*Worcestershire sauce*
2 *tablespoons freshly chopped parsley or half parsley, half chives*	*Drop of Tabasco*
	Salt to taste

Heat the butter in a skillet and add the remaining ingredients. Stir occasionally.

HAMBURGER STEAK

(Serves 6)

2 medium onions, sliced   Fistful of parsley leaves
    thin   2 teaspoons salt
2 tablespoons butter   ¼ teaspoon pepper
3 pounds lean top sirloin   ½ cup water
    of beef

Sauté onion slices in heated butter until well browned and tender. Grind chunks of beef, onions, and parsley through food grinder. Combine with salt, pepper, and water; shape gently into thick patties. Moisten each side of patties slightly with oil and broil 4 inches from tip of flame of a preheated broiler until done the way you like them.

FILET OF BEEF WELLINGTON

(Serves 6)

1 filet of beef, larded with   ½ teaspoon salt
    pork   Dash freshly ground pepper
¼ cup shortening   1 tablespoon chopped
2 cups rich pastry (See   parsley
    note below)   1 tablespoon chopped
1 pound mushrooms   chives, fresh or frozen
1 tablespoon chopped   ¼ cup thick BASIC CREAM
    shallots   SAUCE
1 tablespoon chopped   MADEIRA SAUCE
    onions   Truffles (optional)
1 tablespoon butter

Have the whole filet covered with thin larding pork tied with string. Place filet in a shallow baking pan in the melted shortening. Roast, uncovered, in a preheated 450° F (or very hot) oven for 25 minutes. If the filet is small (2 to 2½ pounds) roast only 15 minutes. Remove from oven and allow to cool.

Prepare the pastry and refrigerate while you make the *duxelles* (mushroom filling).

Wipe mushrooms with a damp cloth, then work through a grinder or blend in an electric blender or chop very, very fine. Cook shallots and onions in heated butter for a minute or so. Stir in mushrooms and cook over a low heat until all liquid has disappeared and mushrooms are dark in color. Stir frequently. Remove from heat, season with salt, pepper, parsley, and chives. Lastly, stir in thick Cream Sauce thoroughly. Cool.

Roll pastry so it is large enough to cover the filet entirely. Lift beef from roasting pan and put a thick covering of the *duxelles* over the surface. Wrap beef in the pastry securely. Bake in a preheated 450° F or very hot oven for 15 to 20 minutes or until pastry is golden brown.

Serve in thickly cut slices with Brown Madeira Sauce mixed with chopped truffles (truffles optional).

Note: A pie-crust mix, prepared according to package directions, will produce an adequate but less rich pastry.

SLICED BEEF TENDERLOIN A LA DEUTSCH
(Serves 4 to 6)

6 *tablespoons butter*
2 *pounds beef tenderloin, sliced ½ inch thick*
2 *medium onions, chopped*
10 *large mushrooms, sliced*
2 *green peppers, thinly sliced*

1 *can (8 ounces) brown gravy*
2 *tablespoons tomato paste*
½ *cup dry sherry*
1 *teaspoon salt*
¼ *teaspoon pepper*
Chopped parsley

In a large frying pan heat butter until it bubbles. Add beef and sauté over a brisk heat until nicely browned on both

sides. Transfer meat to a warm platter. Add onions to same
pan and cook several minutes, stirring frequently. Now stir
in mushrooms and peppers and cook a few minutes. Add
brown gravy, tomato paste, sherry, salt, and pepper. Bring to
a boil and cook several minutes (don't overcook). Sprinkle
with chopped parsley and serve with boiled potatoes or *pasta*.

FILET OF PRIME BLACK ANGUS
[*Beef sauté Marchand de Vin*]

(Serves 4)

5 tablespoons butter, divided
¼ cup finely chopped
  shallots
¾ cup dry red wine
Dash black pepper
1 can (10¾ ounces)
  brown beef gravy or 1¼
  cups

5 tablespoons diced beef
  bone marrow
1½ pounds filet of beef in
  slices about ½ inch thick,
  trimmed
1 tablespoon chopped
  parsley

Heat 2 tablespoons butter in a saucepan. Stir in shallots
and cook slowly for about 5 minutes. Pour in wine, add pepper, and cook until liquid is reduced to one third. Stir in beef
gravy and boil a minute or two. Remove from heat, beat in
1 tablespoon butter and the beef marrow. Taste and add
salt, if needed. Set aside and keep warm.

Melt remaining 2 tablespoons butter in a large skillet.
When butter is bubbling hot, drop in as many slices of the
beef as pan will hold comfortably and sauté quickly. About
2 minutes per side for rare to medium rare; 2 to 3 minutes
longer for well-done beef. Place cooked filets on hot platter,
sprinkle with salt and pepper; keep warm. Before serving,
spoon sauce over the meat and scatter chopped parsley over
all.

SPAGHETTI WITH MEAT SAUCE BOLOGNESE
(Serves 4)

Ingredients for Sauce:

3 *tablespoons butter*

2 *medium-size onions, chopped fine*

4 *fresh cloves of garlic, puréed (or squeezed through garlic press)*

1 *pound coarsely chopped lean beef (chuck)*

1 *small bay leaf*

Salt and pepper to taste

1 *tablespoon flour*

4 *fresh tomatoes, peeled, seeded, and chopped*

2 *tablespoons tomato paste*

2 *cups of water or bouillon*

Heat butter in saucepan, add chopped onions and garlic; sauté 8 to 10 minutes over medium fire until lightly browned. Add the beef, bay leaf; season with salt and pepper. Mix well and sauté all together 10 minutes, stirring often. Blend in the flour, add both the tomatoes and tomato paste. Mix well, then add the water or bouillon. Bring to boil, stirring. Cover and let cook 40 to 50 minutes. Remove bay leaf, season sauce to taste and pour over buttered hot spaghetti. Or serve in separate dish with grated cheese on the side.

BRISKET OF CORNED BEEF AND CABBAGE

Submerge brisket in cold water and heat water as close as possible to the boiling point. Do not allow water to "gallop." Cook the beef at simmering heat from 4 to 5 hours, depending on size. The meat is cooked when a fork easily penetrates the thickest part.

When the beef is thoroughly cooked place it in a vessel of cold water, fat-side down. The size of this vessel should, if possible, be such that the beef will cover the bottom. Use just enough water to cover the meat. Allow to remain in water 15 to 20 minutes. This procedure bleaches the fat and seals in the juices. The heat of the beef will bring up the temperature of the water so the meat will be ready to serve. Trim off excess fat. Carve thin the long way, across the grain and arrange over boiled potatoes and cabbage.

To Prepare the Cabbage:

Select loose green heads of young cabbage. Quarter. Wash thoroughly. Cook in boiling, slightly salted water for 15 to 20 minutes, or until tender. *Do not overcook.*

BAKED CORNED BEEF

Take a hot corned-beef brisket that has been cooked according to directions for BRISKET OF CORNED BEEF AND CABBAGE. Dry the surface thoroughly, then cover with granulated or brown sugar. Place in roasting pan, filled with just enough water to prevent meat from drying out. Bake in a moderate oven of 350° F. When brisket begins to brown, baste with half a cup of fruit juice. Baking time, if brisket is hot, 35 to 40 minutes; if brisket is cold, 60 to 65 minutes.

Note: For a traditional New England boiled dinner, arrange hot slices of corned beef over boiled cabbage. Serve with slices of salt pork garnished with boiled potatoes, baby beets, whole small carrots, and boiled silver onions.

MINCED MILK-FED VEAL SUISSESSE
(Serves 6)

3 *pounds veal, cut from leg, in thin strips*

2 *sticks (1 cup) butter, divided*

1 *tablespoon flour*

1½ *teaspoons salt*

1 *teaspoon paprika*

3 *tablespoons finely chopped shallots or onions*

10 *large mushrooms, sliced thin*

½ *cup dry white wine*

½ *cup heavy cream*

⅔ *cup* BASIC BROWN SAUCE

Have your butcher flatten the meat to a thickness of about
¼ inch, then cut into ¼-✕-1½-inch strips.

Melt two thirds of the butter in a very large, heavy frying
pan, stir in flour, salt and paprika until smooth. Then add
all the meat, bring to a high heat, and cook for 10 minutes.
Stir occasionally. Remove meat and juices to a deep, heavy
pan (a flameproof casserole you can take to the table would
be ideal). Now add remaining butter to frying pan, add shallots or onions and brown lightly for a few minutes. Add
mushrooms and sauté for about 5 minutes, then the wine
and simmer for a few minutes. Combine with meat and stir
in heavy cream and Basic Brown Sauce. Bring to a boil, stirring frequently. Turn down heat and cook for 10 minutes.
Taste for seasoning.

Serve in heated casserole or deep platter with buttered EGG
NOODLES, RICE PILAF, or sautéed potatoes.

STUFFED VEAL CHOPS JURASSIENNE
[Côté de Veau Farci Jurassienne]

(Serves 6)

2 cups BASIC CREAM SAUCE	12 large mushrooms, sliced
Paprika	thin
Sherry	6 thin slices Parma or
6 veal chops	Virginia ham
Salt and pepper	6 thin slices imported
Flour	Swiss cheese
¼ pound butter, divided	

Prepare the Cream Sauce and season with a pinch of paprika and a generous dash of sherry. Set aside and keep warm.
Sprinkle veal chops with salt and pepper; dust lightly with
flour and sauté in 6 tablespoons heated butter in a large skillet. Fry over a low heat until chops are nicely browned on
both sides, about 15 to 20 minutes. While chops cook, sauté

mushrooms in a separate pan, using remaining 2 tablespoons of butter. Mushrooms take about 5 to 6 minutes. Transfer chops to a flameproof platter. Put ham slices into skillet in which the chops sautéed and fry a minute or so. Place a slice of ham on each chop. Top with a heaping spoonful of mushrooms. Cover with a slice of cheese and broil in a preheated broiler until cheese melts. Serve with some of the hot Basic Cream Sauce over each chop.

OSSO BUCO

(Serves 6)

6 veal shanks
Salt and pepper
3 tablespoons flour
3 tablespoons shortening or
    vegetable oil
2 medium onions, chopped
    fine
3 garlic cloves, crushed
3 carrots, diced fine

1 stalk celery, diced fine
4 tomatoes, skinned,
    coarsely chopped
2 bay leaves
Pinch thyme
1 tablespoon tomato paste
1 cup dry white wine
½ cup water
Chopped parsley

Sprinkle veal shanks with salt and pepper, dust with flour, and brown on all sides in heated shortening or vegetable oil. Add onions, garlic, carrots, and celery; simmer over a low heat for 10 to 15 minutes, stirring occasionally. Stir in tomatoes, bay leaves, thyme, tomato paste, wine, and water. Cover tightly and bake in a preheated 350° F (or moderate) oven for 1 hour or until veal is tender when tested with a fork.

Taste for seasoning and add more salt and pepper if needed. Sprinkle parsley over meat and sauce before serving with mashed potatoes, spaghetti, rice, or BAKED CREAM OF WHEAT WITH PARMESAN.

STUFFED VEAL CHOPS, BAKED IN PAPER
[*Côtes de Veau en Papillottes*]

(Serves 6)

6 *veal chops*
Salt and pepper
Flour
4 *tablespoons butter, divided*
1 *tablespoon butter,*
  melted
12 *large mushroom caps,*
  sliced thin
½ *cup boiled ham (about*
  2 *slices), cut in thin strips*

½ *cup calf's tongue (half*
  a 6-ounce jar), cut in thin
  strips
2 *large or 3 medium*
  truffles, sliced thin
  (*optional*)
½ *cup sherry*
1 *can (7½-ounce size)*
  beef gravy

Slash the fat on edges of chops, then season with salt and pepper; dust lightly with flour. Melt 2 tablespoons butter in a large, heavy skillet, add the chops and sauté over medium heat for 25 minutes or until tinged with gold and well done. Turn once. Remove chops from skillet and keep hot.

Add remaining 2 tablespoons butter to same skillet and sauté mushrooms for a few minutes. Then add ham, tongue, and truffles; turn over a few times. Finally, add sherry and gravy. Bring to a boil, scraping bottom and sides to loosen any clinging particles. Then reduce heat and simmer for a few minutes. Taste for seasoning.

While chops cook, cut six heart-shaped pieces of waxed paper to fit each chop, allowing 2 inches overlap all around. Butter one side of the paper with melted butter. When mushroom mixture is cooked, place a chop on buttered side of each piece of paper. Spoon some of the mixture on top of each chop, dividing it evenly among the six. Fold the paper over and roll the edges on the bias as you would a hem, sealing the "package" so that the steam and juices cannot escape. Butter the tops, place in a shallow, buttered baking dish and bake in a preheated moderate or 350° F oven for twenty minutes or until the paper browns somewhat and swells up like little balloons. Remove paper and serve at once.

SCALLOPINI OF VEAL AU MARSALA

(Serves 6)

2 *pounds veal, cut in 12*
  slices and pounded thin
Salt and pepper
Flour
6 *tablespoons butter, divided*
2 *tablespoons chopped*
  shallots

1 *cup Marsala wine*
¾ *cup brown gravy*
  (7½-ounce can)
Chopped parsley

Sprinkle each piece of veal with a little salt and pepper, then coat lightly with flour.

Heat about a third (or 2 tablespoons) of the butter in a heavy skillet and fry the veal, a few pieces at a time, quickly over a high heat, turning once. The meat should be a pretty brown. Keep the cooked veal warm while you do the rest. Add butter as you need it. When all the veal is cooked, add shallots to pan and sauté until they are nicely browned. Then add the Marsala wine and gravy and simmer 2 to 3 minutes, stirring until sauce is smooth and slightly thickened.

Arrange veal on a hot platter, pour sauce over all and sprinkle generously with chopped parsley. Serve with spaghetti, EGG NOODLES, rice, or mashed potatoes.

VEAL CUTLET ORLOFF

(Serves 6)

6 tablespoons mushroom
  purée
6 veal scallopini
Salt and pepper
Flour
4 tablespoons butter,
  divided

6 slices foie gras
6 slices black truffles
6 thin slices Gruyère or
  imported Swiss cheese
2 cups BORDELAISE SAUCE
  (See note below)

To prepare the mushroom purée:

Chop 1 pound mushrooms very fine. Chop 6 shallots very fine and sauté them in 1 tablespoon melted butter for several minutes. Stir in mushrooms along with ½ teaspoon salt and a dash of pepper, several sprigs of finely chopped parsley. Cook over a low heat, stirring frequently, until the mixture is almost dry. This takes from 20 to 25 minutes. Last of all stir in 1 tablespoon butter.

To prepare the cutlets:

Sprinkle veal with salt and pepper. Dust lightly with flour and sauté in remaining butter until golden brown on both sides. Transfer to a flameproof platter. On each piece of veal lay a slice of *foie gras*, then a slice of truffle. Cover with mushroom purée. Top with a slice of Gruyère. Place in a pre-heated broiler until cheese is melted. Serve with half the Bordelaise Sauce around the cutlets and remaining sauce in a separate dish.

Note: A quick Bordelaise can be made by combining 1 can of beef gravy with the same amount of red wine. Heat the mixture until slightly thick.

BREADED VEAL CUTLETS PARMIGIANO

(Serves 4)

4 *veal cutlets, pounded thin*
Flour
2 *eggs, slightly beaten*
Salt and pepper
1 *cup dry bread crumbs* or
  cracker crumbs
¼ *cup butter*

2 *cups* STEWED FRESH
  TOMATOES (See note
  below)
8 *thin slices Mozzarella*
  cheese
½ *cup grated Parmesan*
  cheese

Dust the veal with flour, dip into eggs, season with a sprinkling of salt and pepper. Coat each side with crumbs. Sauté meat in heated butter over a low heat or until golden brown on each side—this takes about 10 minutes. Cover bottom of an ovenproof platter with a little more than half of the tomatoes. Arrange veal on top, covering each cutlet with the remaining tomatoes and 2 slices of Mozzarella. Sprinkle grated Parmesan over the Mozzarella and bake in a preheated 450° F (or hot) oven, for several minutes or until the cheese is thoroughly melted.

Note: Stewed canned tomatoes may be used instead of freshly cooked ones.

VEAL CUTLETS GRUYERE

(Serves 6)

6 *veal cutlets, pounded as*
  for scallopini
Flour
2 *eggs*
2 *tablespoons light cream*
¾ *teaspoon salt*

Dash pepper
2 *cups fine bread crumbs*
6 *tablespoons butter*
6 *thin slices imported*
  Swiss cheese

Coat each thin slice of veal with flour. Dip in a mixture of eggs, cream, salt, and pepper (beaten together slightly). Then coat the cutlets with bread crumbs.

Sauté cutlets in melted butter, over a low heat, until well browned on both sides. Lay a slice of Swiss cheese on each cutlet and put under a preheated broiler until cheese melts and takes on a little color.

Serve with TOMATO SAUCE.

VEAL CUTLETS CORDON BLEU

(Serves 4)

8 *veal scallopini*	2 *eggs, well beaten*
4 *thin slices ham,*	1½ *cups fine dry crumbs*
Prosciutto or Virginia	*Salt and pepper*
4 *thin slices Swiss cheese*	½ *cup butter*
2 *tablespoons flour*	16 *canned asparagus tips*

Place 4 veal scallopini on a tray or heavy board. Place on each a slice of ham, then a slice of cheese. Neither ham nor cheese should extend beyond the edges of the meat. Cover with a second veal scallopini and pound the edges of the meat together with a heavy saucer. Coat with flour, then with eggs, and, finally, with crumbs. Salt and pepper to taste.

Heat butter in a large skillet, add veal and sauté over a moderate heat until golden brown (about 4 to 5 minutes), turn with a broad spatula and brown second side for the same length of time. Serve with drained and heated asparagus tips on top. Garnish with water cress or parsley.

ROAST RACK OF PORK WITH APPLES AND RAISINS, NORMANDE

(Serves 4 to 6)

1 rack of pork (4 to 5
pounds), trimmed, plus
all fat and bones
Salt and pepper
3 carrots, coarsely chopped
2 medium onions, coarsely
chopped
4 or 5 celery leaves, coarsely
chopped
Few sprigs parsley
2 garlic cloves, crushed

½ teaspoon dried thyme
½ teaspoon dried marjoram
4 whole cloves
12 peppercorns, crushed
3 medium tomatoes,
quartered, or 2
tablespoons tomato paste
1 cup dry white wine
1 cup water
1 tablespoon cornstarch

Rub the pork with salt and pepper, place in roasting pan with bones and all the fat trimmings, and roast in a preheated 400° F (or moderately hot) oven for 35 to 40 minutes. Drain off any fat, add carrots, onions, celery leaves, parsley, garlic, thyme, marjoram, cloves, and peppercorns. Continue roasting at same temperature for another 30 minutes. Then reduce oven heat to 325° F (or slow) and roast another 35 minutes. Baste occasionally.

At the end of this cooking period, add tomatoes or tomato paste (fresh tomatoes are best), the cup of wine, and cook 30 minutes longer. Remove meat from roasting pan and keep warm.

To make the gravy, add 1 cup of water to drained roasting pan, bring to a boil; then simmer, scraping and stirring the mixture well to incorporate all the rich brown particles from the pan. When gravy has cooked down somewhat, stir in cornstarch mixed with a little white wine or water. Continue cooking until it has thickened. Strain into a saucepan. Bring to a boil and cook a little longer. If there seems to be an excess of fat, skim it off or suck it up with a baster. Pour gravy into warm sauceboat.

Serve with apples and raisins:

¼ cup raisins	2 to 3 tablespoons sugar
6 green cooking apples	Small pinch cinnamon
4 tablespoons butter	Grated rind of 1 lemon

While pork is roasting prepare the apple-and-raisin mixture. Place the raisins in a small bowl with enough boiling water to cover and let them stand to plump up. Wash and peel apples. Slice. Melt butter in a large skillet. Add apples. Sprinkle with sugar and cinnamon. Then turn the apple slices carefully to coat them with the other ingredients. Cover tightly and let simmer over a low heat from 10 to 15 minutes or until tender. Apple slices should retain their shape. When cooked sprinkle in the lemon rind and the raisins, thoroughly drained. Serve warm or cool with the pork.

PORK CHOPS SAUTE PIQUANTE

(Serves 4)

8 lean pork chops, ½ inch thick	1 cup (7¾-ounce can) brown gravy
Salt and pepper	2 tablespoons mustard (half dry, half French)
2 tablespoons butter	
1 medium onion, chopped	2 tablespoons vinegar
1 tablespoon flour	½ cup finely chopped gherkin pickles
1 cup dry white wine	

Sprinkle pork chops with salt and pepper. Sauté in heated butter, using a low heat, for about 20 minutes or until chops are brown on both sides and cooked through thoroughly. Transfer to a platter and set aside.

Stir onion into the same pan and cook until tender. Add flour and cook a few minutes longer. Gradually mix in wine, brown gravy, and both kinds of mustard. Cook, stirring constantly, until smooth and thick. Now add vinegar and gherkins. Taste sauce and correct seasoning. Return chops to the sauce and simmer 3 to 5 minutes to heat through.

BROCHETTE OF PORK TENDERLOIN

(Serves 4)

8 *large mushroom caps*
6 *tablespoons butter, divided*
1½ *pounds lean pork*
   tenderloin, cut in 1½-inch
   cubes

8 *slices bacon, cut into*
   1½-inch squares
Salt and pepper
½ *cup fresh bread crumbs*

Sauté mushroom caps in 2 tablespoons butter for several minutes, then thread mushrooms, pork cubes, and bacon squares alternately on 4 skewers. Melt remaining 4 tablespoons butter and brush over meat and mushrooms. Place about 4 inches from tip of preheated broiling unit and broil about 10 minutes, turning several times. Sprinkle with bread crumbs and continue broiling and turning until nicely browned and pork is tender when tested with a fork. Serve on a bed of rice with SAUCE DIABLE.

LAMB STEW PARISIENNE

(Serves 6)

3 *pounds lean lamb (leg or shoulder)*

3 *tablespoons shortening*

2 *teaspoons salt*

¼ *teaspoon pepper*

2 *tablespoons flour*

3 *tablespoons tomato paste*

Few sprigs parsley

Few sprigs celery leaves

2 *bay leaves*

Sprig thyme or ¼ teaspoon dried thyme

4 *cloves garlic*

12 *small white onions*

4 *white turnips, medium size*

4 *carrots*

1 *cup cut green beans*

1 *cup fresh peas*

12 *small new potatoes, peeled*

Parsley or chives

Cut lamb into 1½-inch cubes and brown all sides in heated shortening. Now pour off any excess fat and set fat aside. Season lamb with salt and pepper, stir in flour and continue cooking until flour is brown. Add tomato paste and enough water to cover all but one third of the meat. Cook to a boil, stirring constantly. Add parsley, celery leaves, bay leaves, sprig of thyme, all tied together in a bouquet, and garlic. Cover and cook over a low heat.

In the reserved fat, sauté the whole onions, chunks of turnips and carrots until lightly browned. Add to stew. After 40 minutes of cooking, add green beans, fresh peas, and peeled potatoes. Continue cooking until meat and vegetables are tender.

Skim off any excess fat and discard seasoning bouquet and garlic.

Place on hot serving platter and sprinkle with chopped parsley or chives. Lamb should be served very hot.

IRISH LAMB STEW

(Serves 8)

4 *pounds boned shoulder of*
lamb
2 *cups sliced raw potatoes*
¼ *head cabbage, shredded*
4 *leeks, well washed and*
sliced
2 *medium onions, sliced*
1 *stalk celery, sliced*
2 *teaspoons salt*
¼ *teaspoon pepper*
Few sprigs parsley

1 *bay leaf*
2 *cloves garlic, crushed*
¼ *teaspoon dried thyme*
Dash Worcestershire sauce
16 *small white onions*
8 *small carrots*
2 *white turnips, quartered*
1 *pound fresh green peas,*
shelled
Chopped parsley

Cut lamb into 1½-inch cubes. Blanch. Prepare the potatoes, cabbage, leeks, onions, and celery. In a large casserole or baking dish, arrange alternate layers of lamb and the mixed vegetables. Season with salt, pepper, parsley, bay leaf, garlic, and thyme. Add enough water to almost cover mixture and bring to a boil on top of the stove. Cover the casserole and transfer to a preheated 350° F or moderate oven. Bake 1½ hours or until lamb is tender.

Lift meat from casserole to another saucepan and keep warm. Strain liquid from casserole and reserve. Work the mixed vegetables through a sieve or ricer. Now combine puréed vegetables with the liquid and heat to a boil. Stir in Worcestershire sauce and taste to adjust seasoning. Pour sauce over lamb cubes and add cooked onions, carrots, turnips, green peas (these should be cooked while lamb is cooking). Sprinkle stew with chopped parsley. Serve with DUMPLINGS or boiled potatoes.

STUFFED CROWN ROAST OF LAMB
(Serves 8 to 10)

1 *crown roast of lamb, 6 to 7 pounds, as prepared by the butcher*
¼ *cup shortening*

For the mirepoix (which lends flavor to the meat):

2 *onions, cut coarsely*   2 *bay leaves*
2 *carrots, cut coarsely*   6 *cloves*
6 *celery ribs, cut coarsely*   1 *teaspoon of thyme*
4 *crushed garlic cloves*

For the stuffing: (See note below)

2 *pounds equal parts*   3 *cloves of garlic, finely*
  chopped lean lamb, pork,   *chopped*
  and beef   1 *tablespoon butter*
½ *cup white bread crumbs*   ¼ *cup chopped parsley*
2 *eggs*   1 *teaspoon rosemary*
2 *onions, finely chopped*   *Salt and pepper to taste*

Rub the roast well with salt and pepper. Place in a roasting pan with shortening. Fill center of crown with the stuffing. Cover the bones with aluminum foil, to prevent them from charring. Sear roast for 10 minutes in 500° F oven, basting frequently. Turn oven to 375° and roast for 30 minutes, basting every 10 minutes. Add mirepoix and continue cooking 40 to 45 minutes longer. Remove roast to hot serving platter. Discard aluminum foil.

To prepare the gravy, drain the fat from the pan, add 2 cups of water or broth and let boil on top of stove for 10 minutes. Thicken with 1 tablespoon of cornstarch mixed with a little water. Season to taste and strain.

Note: If desired, omit stuffing. Place a cup in the center to keep the crown in shape. Reduce cooking time by 30 minutes.

ROAST LEG OF LAMB LONGCHAMPS

(Serves 6)

1 *leg of lamb* (6 to 7 *pounds*), *plus lamb bones*
Salt *and pepper*
¼ *cup shortening*
2 *medium onions, coarsely chopped*

1 *bay leaf*
2 *carrots, coarsely chopped*
Few *celery leaves, chopped*
¼ *teaspoon dried thyme*
¼ *teaspoon dried oregano*
2 *cups beef broth or water*

Have the butcher send you all bones trimmed from the lamb. Rub the meat with salt and pepper. Next, heat shortening in a roasting pan, add bones and leg of lamb (fat-side up) and roast in a preheated 375° F (or moderate) oven for 30 minutes. At this point add all chopped vegetables mixed with the herbs—distributing them all around the lamb. Continue roasting 35 to 40 minutes longer, basting occasionally. This amount of roasting produces pink lamb (best for flavor and moistness and the way the French cook it), but if you are of the well-done school, roast 20 minutes longer.

Transfer lamb to a heated platter and keep hot.

Pour broth or water (preferably broth) into roasting pan and simmer on top of stove for about 10 minutes. Strain into a saucepan, taste for seasoning, and bring to a boil. Skim off all fat, then pour into warm sauceboat.

Serve with BAKED CREAM OF WHEAT WITH PARMESAN.

BAKED SMOKED HAM CARIBBEAN STYLE

(Serves 10 to 12)

FOR COUNTRY CURED, VIRGINIA OR KENTUCKY-STYLE HAMS:

10- to 12-*pound ham*	1 *cup pineapple juice*
Brown sugar	2 *cans (8-ounce size) brown*
1 *cup Puerto Rico rum,*	*gravy*
divided	

Cover ham with cold water and soak overnight. Next day, drain, cover with fresh water, and simmer over a low heat for about 2½ hours (15 minutes per pound). Remove ham from kettle, trim off rind and part of the fat. Leave about ¼ inch of fat over the surface. Place ham in a shallow baking pan and sprinkle the fatty side with an even coating of brown sugar. Pour in ¾ cup rum and the pineapple juice. Bake in a preheated 375° F (or moderate) oven for 45 to 50 minutes. Baste frequently with the liquids. When ham is handsomely glazed, transfer to a serving platter. Stir the brown gravy into the pan juices and cook to a boil. Skim off all fat. Just before serving add remaining ¼ cup rum. Carve the ham in thin slices and serve the gravy separately.

FOR PRECOOKED, MILD-CURED HAM:

Omit the soaking and simmering steps given above. Just bake a 10- to 12-pound ham in a preheated 325° F (or slow) oven for about 2 hours. At the end of the baking time remove rind and any excess fat. Sprinkle the surface evenly with brown sugar and proceed exactly as for country ham. Bake in a preheated 375° F (or moderate) oven for 30 minutes to glaze. Prepare gravy the same as for country ham.

HAM STEAK WITH GLAZED PINEAPPLE HAWAII

(Serves 6)

2 *large ham steaks, about ½*	6 *slices of canned pineapple*
inch thick	*Pineapple syrup*
2 *tablespoons sugar*	6 *maraschino cherries*

Cut each slice of ham into three servings, slash surrounding fat with a knife to prevent ham from curling, and place on a broiling pan. Sprinkle with a little sugar and broil about 4 inches from preheated broiling unit until temptingly brown on both sides (take care not to broil too much because it dries out). Broil the pineapple following the same directions. Now place a slice of pineapple on each piece of ham, sprinkle with a little pineapple syrup to keep it moist and broil a minute or two longer. Place a cherry in center of each pineapple slice and serve with CANDIED SWEET POTATOES.

MACARONI AU GRATIN WITH HAM

(Serves 4 to 6)

2 *cups macaroni*	¼ *pound ham, slivered*
2 *cups* BASIC CREAM SAUCE	4 *tablespoons butter, divided*
1 *cup light cream*	⅓ *cup grated Parmesan*
1 *teaspoon salt*	*cheese*
Pinch pepper	⅓ *cup grated Swiss cheese*
Pinch nutmeg	

Cook macaroni in a large amount of boiling salted water. When tender, drain thoroughly and mix with Cream Sauce, light cream, salt, pepper, and nutmeg. Sauté ham in 2 tablespoons butter for several minutes, then combine with macaroni.

Transfer to a large buttered baking dish. Sprinkle top with

both grated cheeses and dot with remaining 2 tablespoons butter. Bake in a preheated 350° F (or moderate) oven for 30 to 35 minutes or until golden.

BROILED SWEETBREADS WITH HAM AND MUSHROOMS

(Serves 4)

2 *pairs of sweetbreads*	4 *tablespoons fresh bread*
Salt	*crumbs*
Juice of 1 lemon	8 *mushroom caps*
6 *tablespoons melted butter,*	4 *slices boiled ham*
divided	4 *slices toast*
Pepper	

Soak sweetbreads in cold water for several hours, then drain. Cover with fresh water, seasoned with a little salt and juice of 1 lemon. Cook to a boil, reduce heat and simmer gently for 10 to 12 minutes. Let cool in the liquid, drain, and split each sweetbread through the center. Roll in 4 tablespoons melted butter, sprinkle with salt, pepper, and fresh bread crumbs. Broil about 4 inches from tip of preheated broiler until golden brown on both sides.

While sweetbreads broil, sauté mushroom caps in remaining 2 tablespoons heated butter for several minutes.

To serve, place a slice of ham on a piece of toast, cover with 2 sweetbread halves, and top with SAUTEED FRESH MUSHROOMS. Pour any remaining melted butter over all.

CALVES' BRAINS AU BEURRE NOIR

(Serves 4)

2 *pairs of calves' brains*	Flour
1 *onion, sliced*	4 *tablespoons butter, divided*
1 *bay leaf*	2 *tablespoons vinegar*
5 *whole cloves*	1 *tablespoon capers*
2 *tablespoons white vinegar*	1 *tablespoon chopped parsley*
1 *tablespoon salt*	

Cover brains with cold water and soak for about 1 hour, then remove all veins and membrane. Combine 1 quart of water with onion, bay leaf, cloves, white vinegar, and salt; bring to a boil. Add brains and cook over a low heat for 8 to 10 minutes. Remove from heat and cool right in the broth. When cool, drain and pat dry with paper towels.

Split brains in halves, sprinkle with salt and coat lightly with flour. Sauté in 2 tablespoons heated butter until golden brown on both sides. Transfer to a hot platter. In the same pan heat remaining 2 tablespoons butter until it turns dark brown. Remove from heat and stir in vinegar. Sprinkle capers over the brains, pour the sizzling butter mixture over all, and shower with parsley. Serve with boiled potatoes and leaf spinach, simply cooked.

SAUTEED CALVES' LIVER A LA DEUTSCH

(Serves 6)

1 *quart* BASIC BROWN SAUCE	⅔ *cup white wine*
(See note below)	2¼ *pounds calves' liver,*
½ *cup butter, divided*	*sliced ¼ inch thick and*
2 *large onions, chopped fine*	1½ *inches wide*
2 *green peppers, chopped fine*	Salt and pepper
1 *pound mushrooms, sliced thin*	

Make the sauce first. Heat half the butter in a saucepan. Add onions, green peppers, and mushrooms; cook over a low heat for about 15 minutes. Stir occasionally. Add wine and continue cooking until liquid is reduced to half. Now pour in Brown Sauce, bring to a boil, reduce heat and cook gently for 10 minutes. Keep sauce hot while liver is sautéed.

In a large, heavy skillet heat remaining butter until it turns light brown in color. Add strips of liver and sauté over a high heat tossing them about a few times until meat is medium rare. Liver should not lose any juices during cooking, so make sure temperature is high.

Remove liver from heat, season with salt and pepper, and mix into the hot sauce.

Serve with boiled potatoes, rice, or EGG NOODLES.

Note: Canned gravy can be substituted satisfactorily.

Vegetables

The younger and fresher a vegetable the finer it will be—in appearance, taste, and texture. In Europe the first young vegetables of the season—which menus proudly offer as *primeurs*—are highly prized. It is difficult to get "baby" vegetables here. Our farmers, understandably, choose to let vegetables grow until they have more weight and bring more money.

However, there are fine greengrocers who offer vegetables that are moderately young and very fresh. And any fresh vegetable, even if it is not a *primeur*, is a treat when it is cooked until just tender, drained, and returned to its pan with seasoning and butter added, then moved back and forth over the heat until the seasoning and butter have combined in an appetizing coating.

At Longchamps we insist vegetables be cooked in covered pots with the least possible amount of water so, cooking quickly, they will be neither water-soaked nor mushy nor suffer any serious vitamin loss.

Vegetables must be fresh. From the moment they are picked they slowly lose both vitamins and flavor.

Artichokes are best when their petals are close together and dark green in color.

Asparagus is youngest and freshest when the stalks are crisp and the tips tight.

Beets' freshness can be gauged by the leaves. Beets that are small or medium in size are preferable to those that are large.

Broccoli stalks are tender and the flowers tight and green when broccoli is at its best.

Brussels sprouts show age when they're loosely petaled and oversized instead of having small, tightly closed buds. The fresher sprouts are, the darker green they will be.

Cabbage heads should be compact with fresh crisp leaves.

Carrots should have a brightness of color.

Cauliflower's florets should be white, without blemish, and hold tightly together.

Celery is desirable when the stalks are crisp and the leaves unblemished.

Corn, which deteriorates faster than any other vegetable, should, ideally, be brought from the garden to a boiling pot. The fresher the corn the plumper with milk the kernels will be. At Longchamps, corn is refrigerated the instant it arrives. And it is not husked until it is to go into the boiling water to which a little sugar has been added. When the water reboils, the corn is cooked for exactly four minutes. Both salt and overcooking will toughen corn.

Cucumbers turn seedy as they get larger. Choose those that are of a medium size and firm.

Eggplant is best when it is shiny and smooth, without rust spots.

Green beans and wax beans should have crisp and slender pods.

Lettuce greens, except for a few of the outer leaves, should have compact heads and crisp leaves.

Lima beans are a good buy when their pods are full, crisp, and green.

Mushrooms discolor with age, heat, and handling. Fresh ones are firm and plump and either creamy or slightly ivory-colored.

Okra, when fresh, has crisp and tender pods.

Onions should be hard with a brittle outer skin.

Parsnips, smooth and firm, should be small or medium-sized.

Peas are of an excellence when their green pods are well shaped, smooth, and bright. Peas, like corn, deteriorate quickly. They will be tenderer and sweeter if they are not shelled until they are to be cooked.

Potatoes lose quality when stored more than a week or ten days, even in a cool dark place.

Spinach is best when the leaves are small and dark.

Squash—acorn or butternut—should be oval or round, green, firm, and ridged. Hubbard squash should have wartlike protuberances on a hard rind. And summer squash should have wartlike protuberances on a tender yellow rind.

Tomatoes come in many shades and sizes. But good tomatoes are smooth to the touch without being squashy and without blemish.

Turnips that are light in weight are likely to be pithy and of strong flavor. The fresh ones are heavy and firm.

Zucchini is tenderer and more flavorable when it is small or medium-sized.

Most vegetables are best when boiled until tender, but not beyond this point, and seasoned with salt, pepper, and butter—especially when they are prepared in a pressure cooker. In the recipes that follow, Chef Imhof and I have, therefore, chosen to concentrate on special things: SAUTEED FRESH MUSHROOMS, FRENCH-FRIED ONION RINGS, CORN FRITTERS, STUFFED CABBAGE—never fully appreciated in this country— and tasty variations of potatoes, both sweet and white. For potatoes, which appear every day on most tables, need a little improvisation so they do not become monotonous and, by the same token, unappetizing.

ASSORTED FRESH VEGETABLES [*in pressure cooker*]

(Serves 4 to 6)

6 *leeks*	2 *tablespoons butter*
1 *stalk celery*	2 *onions, sliced thin*
6 *small carrots*	2 *cloves garlic, chopped*
¼ *head green cabbage*	4 *strips bacon, diced*
½ *pound green beans*	*Salt and pepper*
½ *cup fresh peas, shelled*	1 *tablespoon chopped*
4 *medium potatoes*	*parsley*

No liquid is necessary when vegetables are cooked under pressure. Prepare vegetables first: Split leeks lengthwise, wash thoroughly, and cut into 2-inch pieces; cut celery into 2-inch pieces, discarding leaves; scrape carrots and cut into 2-inch chunks; slice cabbage thickly; trim ends from green beans and cut in half, lengthwise; shell peas and measure correct amount; pare potatoes and cut into ½-inch slices.

Heat butter in a pressure cooker. Add onions, garlic, and bacon; sauté until onions are limp but not brown. Add all the vegetables, season with salt and pepper, toss thoroughly. Put cover on pressure cooker, wait until steam puffs out, lower the heat and let cook for 2 to 3 minutes to allow all air in the pot to escape. Put pressure weight on and let rise to the first white marking on the indicator. Lower heat as much as possible and cook 3 more minutes, then remove from heat.

Wait 5 minutes, remove weight, and cover. Return pot to fire and let all liquid evaporate. Serve with a sprinkling of chopped parsley on top. If you haven't a pressure cooker, use a large, heavy saucepan—one with a tight-fitting lid. After all the vegetables are tossed in with the butter-bacon mixture, add ¼ cup boiling water. Cover and cook over a medium heat for 12 to 15 minutes or until vegetables are tender but still on the crisp side.

CORN FRITTERS

(Serves 4)

½ cup fresh or canned kernel
corn
2 eggs, well beaten
½ teaspoon baking powder

2 tablespoons flour
½ teaspoon salt
¼ teaspoon pepper
4 tablespoons shortening

Cut fresh corn off the cob and measure correct amount or, if canned corn is used, drain thoroughly.

Combine corn with eggs, baking powder, flour, salt, and pepper. Heat shortening in a large skillet, drop in batter, a tablespoon at a time, and fry on both sides until puffy and golden.

BRAISED BELGIAN ENDIVE WITH ALMONDS

(Serves 4)

2 tablespoons of butter,
divided
1 carrot, peeled and thinly
sliced
2 to 3 ribs of celery, washed
and thinly sliced
8 to 12 endive heads, washed
and discolored outside
leaves removed

½ teaspoon salt
¼ teaspoon pepper
½ teaspoon sugar
Juice of 1 lemon
1 cup chicken broth
2 tablespoons sliced almonds

In a skillet heat 1 tablespoon of butter. Add sliced carrot and celery and sauté for a few minutes—but do not brown. Arrange the endive over this mixture, season with salt, pepper, and sugar, sprinkle with lemon juice and add chicken broth. Cover with buttered waxed paper. Simmer in oven of 375° F for 30 to 40 minutes or until endive is tender and liquid has been completely reduced. Arrange endive on a hot serving dish. Brown the almonds in remaining butter and spoon over endive.

GREEN PEAS FRENCH STYLE

(Serves 4)

2 *cups fresh green peas, shelled*	2 *slices bacon, sliced thin*
Green leaves of 1 head Boston or romaine lettuce, shredded	½ *cup stock or water*
	Salt and pepper to taste
	1 *teaspoon butter*
8 *small silver onions, parboiled 5 minutes*	1 *teaspoon flour*
	Parsley, freshly chopped

Place all ingredients, except the butter and flour, in boiling water. Cover pan tightly and let simmer for 20 to 30 minutes, or until vegetables are thoroughly cooked. Blend the butter and flour and add to the liquid to thicken. Sprinkle with freshly chopped parsley.

EGGPLANT STEAKS WITH MOZZARELLA AND TOMATOES

(Serves 4)

2 *medium-sized eggplants*	2 *cups peeled, coarsely cut and drained fresh tomatoes*
½ *cup oil*	
Salt and pepper to taste	*Salt and pepper to taste*
1 *large onion, finely chopped*	8 *thin slices Mozzarella cheese*
2 *cloves of garlic, puréed or crushed in garlic press*	
½ *teaspoon basil*	2 *tablespoons of grated Parmesan cheese*

Peel the eggplant and cut into half-inch steaks. Place on oiled baking sheet. Season lightly with salt and pepper and bake in 350° F preheated oven for about 10 minutes, or under the broiler, until tender. Keep hot. Heat remaining oil in a skillet. Add onions, garlic, and basil. Sauté 4 to 5 minutes over low heat. Add the tomatoes, salt, and pepper; cook 15 to 20 minutes.

Arrange the eggplant steaks in a baking dish so they overlap. Cover with tomato mixture. Top with sliced Mozzarella cheese and sprinkle with Parmesan. Broil or bake in hot oven of 475° F, until cheese is melted and brown. Serve at once.

Note: This, an ideal luncheon dish, also can be served on meatless days with anchovy filets.

STUFFED EGGPLANT A L'ITALIENNE

(Serves 4)

2 *medium-size eggplants*
3 *tablespoons salad oil*
2 *tablespoons butter, divided*
1 *small onion, finely chopped*
1 *clove garlic, crushed*
6 *large mushrooms, finely chopped*
½ *cup chopped, cooked ham*
2 *tablespoons dry bread crumbs*
1 *tablespoon chopped parsley*
Salt
Cayenne pepper
2 *tablespoons grated Parmesan cheese*

Trim off the tops and cut unpeeled eggplants in halves, lengthwise. Slash the pulp in several places with a knife. Pour oil in a shallow baking pan, add eggplant halves, cut-side down. Bake in a preheated 375° F (or moderate) oven for 30 to 40 minutes or until tender when tested with a fork. Scoop out eggplant pulp leaving the shell about ¼ inch thick. Chop the pulp and return shells to baking pan.

While eggplants bake, melt 1 tablespoon butter in a saucepan. Add onion and garlic; cook until limp, stir in mushrooms, and continue cooking for 5 minutes. Add ham and simmer gently for 3 to 4 minutes. Remove from heat and blend in bread crumbs, parsley, salt, cayenne, and chopped eggplant pulp. Spoon mixture into shells, sprinkle with remaining tablespoon of melted butter and grated Parmesan cheese. Bake 10 to 12 minutes in a preheated 375° F (or moderate) oven until tops are well browned. Serve hot.

STUFFED CABBAGE

(Serves 6)

1 *large head green cabbage*	½ *teaspoon paprika*
2 *onions, finely chopped*	2 *teaspoons salt, divided*
3 *cloves garlic, finely chopped*	1 *cup tomato juice*
	¼ *cup cider vinegar*
2 *tablespoons butter*	2 *tablespoons sugar*
1 *pound lean ground beef*	2 *cups beef broth or water*
2 *tablespoons chopped parsley*	1 *bay leaf*
½ *cup cooked rice*	¼ *teaspoon pepper*

Leave cabbage head whole but ream out some of the solid core. Cover with boiling salted water and cook 10 minutes. Drain thoroughly. Pull off about 14 to 16 large outer leaves and trim away some of the thick stem. Chop about ¾ cup of the cabbage center to use later on.

Cook onions and garlic together in heated butter for several minutes, then blend thoroughly with chopped beef, chopped cabbage, parsley, rice, paprika, and 1 teaspoon salt. Put about 2 tablespoons of this mixture in the center of each cabbage leaf, roll up, and tuck in the ends. Place in a buttered shallow baking dish. Combine tomato juice, vinegar, sugar, broth or water, bay leaf, pepper, and remaining teaspoon salt. Pour over cabbage rolls, cover tightly, and bake in a preheated 350° F (or moderate) oven for 1½ to 2 hours. Served with boiled potatoes.

RED CABBAGE WITH APPLES

(Serves 4)

2 *tablespoons shortening or*   · 2 *tablespoons sugar*
bacon drippings   1 *teaspoon salt*
1 *large onion, finely chopped*   *Dash pepper*
2 *apples, pared, cored, sliced*   1 *bay leaf*
thin   1 *medium head red cabbage*
1 *cup water*   1 *tablespoon flour*
½ *cup red-wine vinegar*

Heat shortening or drippings in a large saucepan. Add onion and sauté 3 to 4 minutes. Toss in apple slices and cook several minutes longer. Stir in water, vinegar, sugar, salt, pepper, and bay leaf; heat to the boiling point. Shred cabbage as for cole-slaw and mix into vinegar combination. Cover tightly and cook over a low heat for 40 to 45 minutes. Stir occasionally. Just before serving add the flour, stirring constantly, until mixture thickens slightly.

BRAISED BAVARIAN CABBAGE

(Serves 4)

1 *large onion*   1 *teaspoon salt*
2 *tablespoons ham or bacon*   1 *tablespoon sugar*
drippings or shortening   *Dash pepper*
1 *medium head green*   ½ *cup cider vinegar*
cabbage   1 *cup broth or water*
1 *tablespoon caraway seeds*

Cut onion in thin slices and sauté in heated drippings or shortening for about 10 minutes. Use a deep kettle. Stir frequently so that onion does not brown.

Cut cabbage in quarters, remove core, and slice in ½-inch

slices. Add to onion along with remaining ingredients and mix thoroughly. Bring to a boil, cover tightly, and cook gently for 40 to 45 minutes. Serve as an accompaniment to ROAST PORK, SMOKED HAM, or sausage.

STEWED FRESH TOMATOES

(Serves 4 to 5)

12 *ripe large tomatoes*	*Salt and pepper to taste*
2 *tablespoons butter or oil*	*Pinch of sugar*
2 *onions, finely chopped*	1 *tablespoon chopped*
2 *cloves garlic, peeled and*	*parsley*
chopped	

Plunge tomatoes into boiling water for a minute or two, then into cold water. Remove skin. Cut tomatoes in halves, squeeze or scoop out the seeds. Chop tomatoes coarsely. In a saucepan heat the butter or oil, sauté the onions and garlic for 2 to 3 minutes. Add tomatoes, salt, pepper, and sugar. Cook over strong flame until most of the liquid has evaporated. Add coarsely chopped parsley before serving.

FRENCH-FRIED ONION RINGS

(Serves 4)

FIRST METHOD

Cut large sweet onions in slices about ⅛ inch thick (allowing 1 large onion for 2 normal appetites), then separate the slices into rings. Sprinkle with salt and pepper; dip into milk; coat lightly with flour. Fry in deep fat heated to 375° F on fat thermometer (or until an inch cube of bread browns in 40 seconds) for a few minutes until crisp and golden brown. Drain on paper towels and serve immediately.

SECOND METHOD

Cut large sweet onions in slices about ⅛ inch thick, allowing 1 large onion for 2 normal appetites. Separate slices into rings and dust with flour. Dip into FRENCH FRITTER BATTER, then fry in deep fat heated to 375° F on fat thermometer (or until an inch cube of bread browns in 40 seconds) for a few minutes until crisp and golden. Drain on paper towels and serve immediately.

SAUTEED FRESH MUSHROOMS

(Serves 4)

1½ pounds fresh mushrooms
2 tablespoons butter
Salt and pepper to taste

Juice of 1 lemon
1 tablespoon chopped
    parsley

Clean and wash mushrooms thoroughly; dry and slice them thin. Heat butter in a saucepan or skillet and sauté mushrooms quickly over bright flame for 3 to 4 minutes. Season with salt, pepper, and lemon juice. Cook 5 minutes more, shaking the pan occasionally. Before serving add chopped parsley.

CAULIFLOWER POLONNAISE

(Serves 4 to 6)

1 medium-sized cauliflower
Juice of 1 lemon
3 tablespoons of butter
½ cup bread crumbs

2 tablespoons of chopped
    hard-boiled eggs
1 tablespoon freshly chopped
    parsley

Trim the cauliflower of its green leaves and the tough section of the core. Wash thoroughly. Then cook in boiling salted water to which the juice of 1 lemon has been added, from 20 to 30 minutes or until tender. Remove from pot. Drain. Place on hot serving dish. Heat the butter in a frying pan until it is light brown. Add crumbs and toss a few times. Then pour the sizzling butter and crumbs over the cauliflower. Sprinkle with the chopped eggs and parsley.

POTATO GNOCCHI PIEMONTESE

(Serves 4 to 6)

2 pounds potatoes	½ cup mushroom sauce or
1 cup flour	brown gravy
2 whole eggs	¼ cup grated Parmesan
2 egg yolks	cheese
¼ teaspoon salt	4 tablespoons butter, divided
Dash pepper	2 garlic cloves, finely chopped
Dash nutmeg	

Pare potatoes and cook in lightly salted water until tender. Drain thoroughly and while still hot, work through a ricer or mash smoothly. Beat in flour, whole eggs and extra egg yolks, salt, pepper, and nutmeg.

Roll mixture into balls the size of a walnut, then shape into little cylinders. Drop into lightly salted, boiling water and simmer gently for 10 minutes. Remove from water with a perforated spoon, drain thoroughly, and arrange in a buttered baking dish.

Heat mushroom sauce or brown gravy and pour over gnocchi. Sprinkle with grated cheese and 1 tablespoon melted butter. Bake in a preheated 450° F (or hot) oven for 15 to 20 minutes. Before serving, sauté garlic in the remaining butter until golden, pour over gnocchi and serve immediately. More grated Parmesan cheese can be served in a separate dish.

PARISIENNE POTATOES

(Serves 5 to 6)

6 *large peeled potatoes*   *Salt to taste*
¼ *pound of butter*   *Chopped parsley to taste*

Scoop out rounds of potatoes, using a melon-ball cutter. Parboil potato balls in slightly salted water for 2 to 3 minutes. Drain. Heat the butter in a frying pan. Add the potatoes and sauté until golden brown and tender, shaking the pan frequently so the potatoes will brown evenly. Sprinkle with salt and chopped parsley.

WAFFLE POTATOES

Pare as many potatoes as you need—count on 1 medium-sized potato per person. Use a waffle vegetable cutter and cut potatoes into slices. Rinse in hot water, drain, and pat completely dry.

Heat deep fat to 375° F on thermometer (or until hot enough to brown a one-inch cube of bread in 40 seconds). Drop in a handful of potato slices at a time and fry until brown and crisp. Drain on paper towels. Sprinkle with salt.

STUFFED BAKED POTATOES

(Serves 6)

6 *Idaho potatoes*   ¼ *cup heavy cream*
4 *tablespoons butter, divided* 2 *tablespoons finely minced*
1 *chopped onion*   *chives*
3 *strips bacon, cut into small* *Salt, pepper, and nutmeg to*
   pieces   *taste*
2 *tablespoons chopped*   2 *tablespoons grated*
   cooked ham   *Parmesan cheese*

Bake the potatoes in 375° F oven for 50 to 60 minutes, or until done. Cut off ⅓ potatoes lengthwise. Scoop out insides and mash. Keep hot. Heat half the butter in a skillet, add onion, and sauté for few minutes, then add bacon and ham and sauté for few minutes more. Add to this mixture the mashed potatoes and cream, chives, salt, pepper, nutmeg, and 2 teaspoons of butter. Blend well. Spoon mixture into potato shells. Sprinkle with Parmesan cheese and remaining butter, melted. Bake in 400° F oven for approximately 15 minutes.

AU GRATIN POTATOES

(Serves 6)

2 pounds potatoes
2 cups light cream
2 tablespoons butter, divided

Salt and pepper to taste
3 tablespoons grated cheese
2 tablespoons bread crumbs

Cook potatoes in their skins for 30 minutes, or until tender (depending on size) in boiling salted water. Drain, let cool, and then peel. Dice into small pieces. Bring the cream to a boil, add potatoes and half the butter, and let cook about 10 minutes, stirring occasionally, until thick. Season with salt and pepper. Pour into a baking dish, sprinkle with grated cheese and bread crumbs; top with remaining butter. Brown under hot broiler.

LYONNAISE POTATOES

(Serves 4 to 6)

4 tablespoons of butter
1 medium onion, sliced thin
6 medium-sized boiled
potatoes, sliced

Salt and pepper to taste
1 tablespoon chopped parsley

Heat the butter in a large frying pan, add the sliced onion, and sauté for 3 or 4 minutes. Add the sliced potatoes, season with salt and pepper. Brown slowly on both sides. Serve with chopped parsley sprinkled on top.

POTATO CROQUETTES

(Serves 4)

4 medium-sized potatoes	2 whole eggs, well beaten
2 egg yolks	1 cup fine dry bread crumbs
Flour	Fat for deep frying

Pare potatoes and cook in boiling salted water until tender. Drain and work through a ricer or mash smoothly. While potatoes are still hot, beat in the egg yolks. Cool; pat into croquette shapes (pyramid, rounds, or sausagelike). Coat with flour. Dip into whole eggs and cover evenly with crumbs.

Fry in deep fat heated to 375° F until golden and crusty. Drain on paper towels.

POTATO PANCAKES

(Yield: about 24 3-inch cakes)

1 quart coarsely grated potatoes	1 teaspoon salt
	Dash pepper
1 egg	Dash nutmeg
3 tablespoons oil	1 tablespoon grated onion
2 tablespoons flour	Beef fat or butter or bacon fat

Grate potatoes into a bowl of cold water. Drain. Then place in a tea towel and wring out as much liquid as possible. Beat egg lightly and stir in oil, flour, salt, pepper, nutmeg, grated onion, and potatoes. Sauté by spoonfuls in ¼ inch of heated fat over a moderate heat until brown on the bottoms. Turn and brown other sides.

CANDIED SWEET POTATOES

(Serves 6)

6 *good-sized sweet potatoes*   3 *tablespoons syrup* (*Karo*)
3 *tablespoons butter*
2 *tablespoons powdered*
  sugar

Boil the sweet potatoes in their skins in lightly salted water until tender. Drain and let cool. Peel and cut in 1-inch-thick slices. Heat the butter in a skillet and brown potatoes on both sides. Sprinkle with sugar and syrup; arrange in baking dish. Glaze in hot oven for 15 to 20 minutes, basting with syrup from time to time.

SWEET-POTATO SOUFFLE

(Serves 6 to 8)

6 *medium-sized sweet*   1 *teaspoon grated orange*
  potatoes   *rind*
¾ *cup hot milk*   4 *egg whites*
¼ *cup butter*

Cook potatoes in their skins until tender. Drain, peel, and mash them. Beat in the hot milk, butter, and grated orange rind. Season with salt to taste. Beat until mixture is fluffy. Fold in egg whites, beaten until they form peaks. Pour mixture into well-buttered soufflé dish. Bake in 375° F oven for 35 to 40 minutes, until golden brown.

Dumplings · Matzoh Balls · Rice · Baked Cream of Wheat with Parmesan · Pasta · Pancakes

Little extra touches can make a world of difference, not only to the dish they embellish, but to the interest they lend an over-all menu.

IRISH LAMB STEW, for instance, isn't really Irish lamb stew unless DUMPLINGS, light and fluffy, await its particularly appetizing gravy.

CURRIED FRESH SEAFOOD CALCUTTA—like many other dishes—has such provocative flavor it is really a pity to serve it without RICE PILAF, every grain of which will hoard the rich sauce.

HUNGARIAN BEEF GOULASH and FILET OF BEEF STROGANOFF—and many similar dishes—are less than they should be unless they are accompanied by golden EGG NOODLES, done to a tender turn.

ROAST LEG OF LAMB LONGCHAMPS is a fine entree. But serve it with squares of well-seasoned BAKED CREAM OF WHEAT WITH PARMESAN, baked to a golden brown, and it is inspired. An Italian food this, known natively as Gnocchi Romaine.

CHICKEN IN BROTH just isn't the true French Pot au Feu Henry IV without MARROW DUMPLINGS or MATZOH BALLS.

Pasta wears many faces, depending upon the color it takes from its flour, the infinite and fascinating shapes and sizes in which it is manufactured, and, last but not at all least, the meat, cheese, or fish with which the larger *pasta* is stuffed and the sauce that is poured over it.

Pancakes need no recommendation to those of us who relish them, buttered and syruped or honeyed, especially on cold winter mornings. But there are pancakes and pancakes. If you've never tried CORN-MEAL PANCAKES, for instance, it's high time to turn a few pages and plan this treat for next Sunday's breakfast.

DUMPLINGS

1 cup flour
½ teaspoon salt
½ teaspoon baking powder
1 egg white
1 tablespoon melted butter
¼ cup milk (about)

Sift together flour, salt, and baking powder. Beat egg white until it holds a shape. Stir into flour mixture, butter and milk, alternately. Add just enough milk to make a soft dough.

Transfer dough to a lightly floured breadboard and pat about ½ inch thick. Cut into little 1½-inch squares and drop in a large shallow pan of boiling salted water. Cover tightly and cook slowly for 7 to 8 minutes. Lift from water with a slotted spoon and serve immediately with the stew.

MARROW DUMPLINGS

(Serves 4)

2 tablespoons beef marrow, strained
2 eggs
½ cup fine white bread crumbs
1 teaspoon chopped parsley
½ teaspoon salt
Dash pepper

Remove uncooked marrow from bones with a spoon or knife (or ask your butcher to do it for you). Heat marrow in a frying pan until melted. Strain and put 2 tablespoons marrow in a bowl. Add well-beaten eggs, then the bread crumbs, parsley, pepper and salt. Refrigerate until mixture is firm enough to roll into balls about ¼ inch in diameter. Heat with dish they are to accompany for about 5 minutes.

MATZOH BALLS

(Serves 4)

4 *eggs, separated*
¾ *cup matzoh meal*
¼ *cup dry bread crumbs*
¼ *cup water*
¼ *cup salad oil*

1 *tablespoon chicken fat*
½ *teaspoon baking soda*
½ *teaspoon salt*
Pinch of nutmeg

Beat egg yolks hard. Then add all remaining ingredients, except egg whites, and mix until well blended. Beat egg whites until frothy (not stiff) and fold into mixture. Refrigerate 15 to 20 minutes. Shape into little balls the size of a walnut.

Heat with dish they are to accompany for about 5 minutes.

RICE PILAF

(Serves 4 to 6)

4 *tablespoons butter, divided*
1 *medium onion, finely chopped*
1 *cup long-grain rice*

3 *cups boiling stock of chicken, veal, or beef* (See note below)

Melt 2 tablespoons butter in a heavy saucepan (one with a tight-fitting lid), stir in onion, and cook several minutes. Do not brown.

Wash rice thoroughly, drain and stir into onion mixture until rice grains are coated with butter. Add boiling stock, cover tightly, and cook over a low heat for 15 to 20 minutes or until stock is all absorbed. Remove from heat and stir in remaining 2 tablespoons of butter.

Note: If no stock is available dissolve 3 bouillon cubes in 3 cups boiling water.

BAKED CREAM OF WHEAT WITH PARMESAN [*Gnocchi Romaine*]

(Serves 6)

1 *quart milk*
1½ *cups cream of wheat or semolina*
3 *eggs, well beaten*
½ *cup grated Parmesan cheese, divided*

1 *teaspoon salt*
¼ *teaspoon white pepper*
Dash nutmeg
¼ *cup melted butter*

Heat milk to boiling point and stir in cereal. Cook over a low heat, stirring frequently, for 12 to 15 minutes. Mixture at this point is very heavy and stiff. Take off the heat and stir in eggs, half the grated cheese, salt, pepper, and nutmeg. Spread evenly on a buttered platter to a depth of about 1 inch. Cool until firm.

Cut into 2-inch squares, place in a buttered shallow baking pan, scatter remaining cheese over the squares and pour a little melted butter over each square. Bake in a preheated 350° F (or moderate) oven for about 20 minutes. If gnocchi isn't golden at this point, slide under the broiler for a minute or so—but watch it.

SPAETZLES

(Serves 6 to 8)

4 *cups sifted all-purpose flour*
1 *teaspoon salt*
Dash of nutmeg

1 *tablespoon oil*
5 *eggs*
1 *cup milk*
¼ *cup butter*

Sift flour, salt, and nutmeg into a bowl, then stir in the oil. Beat eggs soundly, add the milk and, gradually, beat into flour mixture producing a heavy dough. Heat about 2 quarts of salted water to a boil. Work or force the spaetzle dough through a colander—one with large holes—into the boiling water. Cook about 5 minutes or until spaetzles swim to the surface. Remove with a strainer and drain. When dry, heat butter in a skillet until it starts to foam. Add spaetzles and sauté, stirring frequently, until lightly browned. Serve as an accompaniment with stew, pot roast, or sauerbraten.

EGG NOODLES

(Yield: about 1½ pounds)

5 *eggs*	1 *tablespoon salt*
¼ *cup cold water*	4 *cups all-purpose flour*

Combine eggs, water, and salt in a bowl and mix together lightly. Sift flour into a mixing bowl and dig a hole or cavity in the center. Add egg mixture and stir with your hand until well blended. If dough is not extremely stiff at this point, sift in a little additional flour.

Place on a floured board and knead until smooth and elastic. Roll with a floured rolling pin until thin as possible. Lift and turn the dough frequently to prevent sticking. Cover with a tea towel and let stand for about 30 minutes. Cut into two portions and roll up each as you would a jelly roll. Slice into strips as thin or as wide as you wish and shake the slices apart. Let noodles dry before cooking in boiling salted water for 12 to 15 minutes.

GRIDDLE CAKES NO. 1

(Yield: about 10 cakes)

1 *cup all-purpose flour*	2 *eggs*
1 *tablespoon baking powder*	1 *cup milk*
2 *tablespoons sugar*	2 *tablespoons melted butter*
½ *teaspoon salt*	

Sift together in a bowl: flour, baking powder, sugar, and salt. In another bowl beat eggs vigorously. Then stir in milk and melted butter. Combine with dry ingredients, using as few strokes as possible (don't worry about the lumps).

Drop batter by spoonfuls onto a hot, greased griddle. Griddle is the right temperature when a few drops of cold water sprinkled on it dance around. Turn griddle cakes when bubbles appear on the surface and begin to burst. Brown other sides. Serve at once.

GRIDDLE CAKES NO. 2

(Yield: about 36 cakes)

4 *cups all-purpose flour*	5 *cups milk*
3 *tablespoons baking powder*	4 *tablespoons melted butter*
5 *tablespoons sugar*	Grated rind of 2 lemons
1 *teaspoon salt*	4 *tablespoons lemon juice*
3 *eggs, separated*	

Sift together in a bowl: flour, baking powder, sugar, and salt. Beat egg yolks vigorously in another bowl and stir in milk, melted butter, lemon rind, and lemon juice. Combine with dry ingredients, using as few strokes as possible (don't worry about the lumps). Beat egg whites until they hold definite peaks, then fold gently but thoroughly into the batter.

Drop spoonful by spoonful onto a hot, greased griddle. Griddle is the right temperature when a few drops of cold water sprinkled on it dance around. Turn griddle cakes when bubbles appear on the surface and begin to burst. Brown other sides. Serve immediately.

CORN-MEAL PANCAKES

(Yield: about 36 cakes)

1¼ *cups all-purpose flour*	4 *eggs, separated*
2½ *cups corn meal*	1 *quart buttermilk*
1 *teaspoon salt*	¼ *cup melted butter*
2 *tablespoons sugar*	

Sift together in a bowl: flour, corn meal, salt, and sugar. In a separate bowl beat egg yolks vigorously. Stir in buttermilk and melted butter. Combine with dry ingredients, using as few strokes as possible (don't worry about the lumps). Beat egg whites until they hold a peak, then fold into batter gently but thoroughly.

Drop batter by spoonfuls onto a hot, greased griddle. Griddle is the right temperature when a few drops of cold water sprinkled over it bounce and dance around. Turn pancakes when bubbles appear on the surface and begin to burst. When other side is brown, serve immediately.

BUTTERMILK GRIDDLE CAKES

(Yield: about 36 cakes)

3 *cups all-purpose flour*	2 *eggs*
1 *tablespoon baking powder*	2½ *cups buttermilk*
½ *teaspoon salt*	¼ *cup melted butter*
1 *tablespoon sugar*	

Sift together in a bowl: flour, baking powder, salt, and sugar. In a separate bowl beat eggs vigorously. Stir in buttermilk and melted butter. Combine liquid and dry ingredients with as few swift strokes as possible (don't worry about the lumps). Overmixing toughens pancakes.

Drop batter by the spoonfuls onto a hot, greased griddle. Griddle is the right temperature when a few drops of cold water sprinkled on it dance around. Turn griddle cakes when bubbles appear on the surface and begin to burst. When other side is brown, serve immediately.

BUCKWHEAT CAKES

(Yield: about 36 cakes)

1 *package (½ ounce) active dry yeast*	1 *teaspoon salt*
1 *quart milk*	2 *tablespoons molasses*
4 *cups buckwheat flour*	½ *tablespoon baking soda*
	½ *cup warm water*

Sprinkle yeast over warm water to soften. Heat milk until a film shines on top; remove from heat and cool to lukewarm. Combine yeast, milk, buckwheat flour, and salt. Beat hard for several minutes. Cover with a cloth and let stand at room temperature overnight. Next morning, stir in molasses, baking soda, and ½ cup water.

Drop by spoonfuls onto a hot, greased griddle. Griddle is the right temperature when a few drops of cold water sprinkled over it dance around. Turn buckwheat cakes when bubbles appear on the surface and begin to burst. When other sides are brown, serve immediately.

Salads and Salad Dressings

The difference between an appetizing and refreshing salad and a limp and insipid concoction which deserves to be damned as "rabbit's food," lies, almost always, in trifles.

Whatever the salad greens—there are over thirty kinds—they should be washed, preferably with a spray. If a salad basket is used, it should be commodious enough so, without bruising a single leaf, it can be swung briskly—until the last drop of water falls away. Oil and water, you will remember, do not mix.

The next step in making a salad is to pour oil over the greens that have been turned out, crisp and dry, into a large bowl which, depending upon personal preference and a salad's ingredients, has been rubbed well, slightly, or not at all, with garlic.

Then, after a sprinkling of salt and as much fresh black pepper as a few turns of a pepper mill will yield, a salad is tossed until the oil coats every leaf so that the vinegar which follows will not bite into any unprotected green and leave it with a bite in flavor.

Trifling, all of this! But should I find a *garde-manger*, who is the salad chef, neglectful of any one of these details I would, at once, look for another *garde-manger*. For the result to which these trifles add up is not trifling at all.

Usually, salad is served separately after a main course.

In California it is sometimes served as a first course.

I prefer my salad served with the meat, poultry, or fish—with which it should, of course, be companionable—so there may be a give and take of flavor.

Cold roast beef is at its finest when it is accompanied by a salad of spinach leaves, coarsely chopped carrot, beets marinated for an hour or two or three in good, old-fashioned cider vinegar and—just before the benediction of the oil, seasonings, and vinegar—sprinkled generously with finely minced celery leaves.

Duck is more flavorful with a salad of orange and avocado slices on a bed of water cress with a faintly sweet French dressing.

Other birds: chicken, turkey, goose, guinea hen, pheasant, Cornish hen—hot or cold—get a boost in flavor when they're served with Bibb or romaine and a half peach filled with a good chutney.

Curried dishes respond to a salad of endive, crisp diced apple, celery stalks, and a few broken nuts or raisins, perhaps, but, definitely, with a touch of sharp, dry mustard in the FRENCH DRESSING.

Ham quickens in taste with a salad of spinach leaves, chopped scallions, and onions or pineapple.

Mixed green salads, the gourmets' favorite, lack only one thing—an appetizing contrast in color. This lack can be corrected, simply and quickly, with no detriment to the salad, by a few carrot curls or tiny balls of Roquefort rolled in celery seed.

The more interest and imagination that goes into the preparation of any food the better it is likely to be. But with salads this is exaggeratedly true.

The salads that follow are those which are most often ordered at the Longchamps restaurants to complement a main dish or as a luncheon or supper entree. Chef Imhof and I found it difficult to know where to stop in giving dressing directions. For it is our experience that the dressing that best suits any salad combination is something that must be decided by individual taste.

TROPICAL PINEAPPLE BASKET WITH CHICKEN SALAD HOME STYLE

(Serves 6)

3 pineapples, cut in halves and cored
6 cups chicken salad
6 tablespoons thick MAYONNAISE
6 oranges, separated into sections
4 grapefruit, separated into sections

12 scoops of Cranshaw and Honeydew melons
½ basket blueberries
6 large strawberries
6 tablespoons shredded coconut

Fill cored pineapple halves with 1 cup chicken salad each. Spread Mayonnaise over salad, arrange orange and grapefruit sections alternately. Garnish with melon balls and blueberries. Top each with strawberry. Sprinkle with shredded coconut. Serve on lettuce leaves.

CHILLED STUFFED TOMATO MA FACON

(Serves 4)

4 good-sized, firm, ripe tomatoes
2 cups diced chicken
¼ cup diced celery

1 tablespoon chopped sweet-sour gherkins
½ cup MAYONNAISE
½ teaspoon curry powder

GARNISHES

4 slices hard-boiled egg
12 scoops avocado pear

Scald and peel tomatoes. Cut off tops. Scoop out pulp and seeds. Season inside of tomatoes with a little salt and stuff them with chicken salad. Cover salad with small amount of Mayonnaise. Top with a slice of hard-boiled egg. Garnish with scoops of avocado pear.

Serve, very cold, on shredded lettuce with a bouquet of water cress. Pass, separately, additional Mayonnaise and thin slices of pumpernickel.

ADDITIONAL SUGGESTIONS FOR FILLINGS

Tuna fish mixed with coarsely diced hard-boiled egg, topped with vinaigrette sauce and garnished with cucumber slices.

Lobster, crabmeat, or shrimp salad prepared with TARTAR SAUCE and diced celery. For garnishings use slices of hard-boiled egg and rounds of black olives.

Scoops of cottage cheese, garnished with sections of tangerines (fresh or canned) or oranges, melon balls, and fresh strawberries.

Salmon salad prepared with RUSSIAN DRESSING, diced celery, and finely cut chives. Top with additional Russian dressing. Decorate with small cucumber balls and rolled anchovy filets.

Waldorf salad of diced raw apples and diced raw celery mixed with MAYONNAISE. Garnish with chopped walnuts.

Alaska king crabmeat salad prepared with MAYONNAISE to which a pinch of curry powder has been added. Garnish with slice of king crabmeat topped with shredded coconut.

SPECIAL EXECUTIVE SALAD

(Serves 6)

1 *head romaine*
1 *head Boston lettuce*
1 *head chicory*
1 *head escarole*
24 *fresh jumbo shrimp,*
boiled
6 *breasts of boiled chicken or*
fowl

6 *hard-boiled eggs,*
quartered
6 *small tomatoes, cut in*
wedges
1 *bouquet water cress*
24 *anchovy filets*

Place washed and drained mixed salad greens in a large bowl. Top with alternate arrangement of shrimp and chicken —cut in strips about 2 inches long and ¼ inch thick. Garnish with quartered eggs and tomato wedges.

Place bouquet of water cress and anchovy filets on top.

Pour 1 pint tangy FRENCH DRESSING over all and blend well.

CAESAR SALAD

(Serves 4)

1 *clove of garlic*
3 *heads of romaine*
6 *tablespoons oil*
12 *filets of anchovies*
Worcestershire sauce
Salt and pepper to taste

4 *tablespoons grated*
Parmesan cheese
4 *two-minute soft-boiled eggs*
Juice of 3 lemons
6 *slices white sandwich*
bread

(As a substitute for the oil and lemon juice FRENCH DRESS-ING may be used.)

Rub a wooden salad bowl well with peeled garlic. Wash and dry romaine thoroughly. Trim stem ends, break into pieces 2 inches long, and put into bowl. Add oil, anchovies, a few drops of Worcestershire sauce, salt, pepper, and grated cheese. Add the soft-boiled eggs and lemon juice. Toss lightly with wooden spoon and fork. Top tossed salad with the browned bread cubes (croutons). To prepare: trim the crusts from the bread, cut each slice into small cubes, and brown in oil heavily seasoned with garlic.

This salad should be concocted at table and served immediately.

CUCUMBER SALAD

(Serves 4)

4 *medium cucumbers*	⅓ *cup freshly chopped*
Salt	*parsley*
Oil and vinegar to taste	1 *hard-boiled egg, chopped*
Pepper to taste	

Cut off and discard thick slices from both ends of the cucumbers. Peel and slice thinly into salad bowl. Sprinkle with salt. Place heavy plate on top of cucumbers and let them stand in salt marinade for 1 to 2 hours. When ready to serve, pour off water by pressing the plate over the cucumbers in order to extract all liquid possible. Season with oil, vinegar, and pepper. (Additional salt may be unnecessary.) Sprinkle with chopped parsley and chopped hard-boiled egg.

SPRING SALAD

(Serves 4)

2 *hearts Boston lettuce,*	2 *hard-boiled eggs, chopped*
quartered	⅓ *cup finely chopped chives*
4 *spoonfuls well-seasoned*	⅓ *cup finely chopped*
MAYONNAISE *or* RUSSIAN *or*	*parsley*
FRENCH DRESSING	

Wash the quartered lettuce thoroughly and let stand in very cold water. Drain and dry. Place 2 quarters of lettuce on each individual salad plate. Put 1 spoonful of mayonnaise, Russian or French Dressing over each serving of lettuce. Sprinkle with chopped egg, chives, and parsley.

FRESH-VEGETABLE SALAD

(Serves 4)

4 cups fresh vegetables	8 small florets cauliflower
Oil and vinegar to taste	1 quartered head of lettuce
Salt and pepper to taste	12 slices cooked beets

Cook vegetables—such as carrots, lima beans, string beans, turnips, peas, and celery—until barely tender. Drain and cool. Then toss them lightly with oil and vinegar, salt and pepper. Place in salad bowl. Garnish with cauliflower, quartered lettuce, sliced cooked beets, or any other vegetable of your choice.

TOMATO SALAD

(Serves 4)

4 medium tomatoes	⅓ cup freshly chopped
Salt and pepper to taste	parsley
Oil and vinegar to taste	2 medium onions

Plunge tomatoes into boiling water for a moment, then into cold water, so they will peel easily. Cut the tomatoes into thin slices and arrange neatly on individual salad plates or on a platter. Season with salt and pepper, oil and vinegar. Let chill and marinate half an hour. Before serving sprinkle with chopped parsley and onions.

COLESLAW—RECIPE NO. 1

(Serves 6 to 8)

1 *head cabbage*
1 *tablespoon salt*
2 *tablespoons sugar*
¼ *cup white vinegar*
Pinch pepper

⅛ *cup finely sliced green*
pepper
⅛ *cup grated raw carrots*
1 *cup* MAYONNAISE
⅓ *cup chopped parsley*

Shred cabbage and marinate for 24 hours in quart of water with salt, sugar, vinegar, and pepper added. Drain cabbage at the end of this time and mix well with green pepper, carrots, and Mayonnaise. Season to taste. Serve with sprinkling of chopped parsley.

COLESLAW—RECIPE NO. 2

(Serves 6 to 8)

Follow the same procedure. But omit mayonnaise, substituting ¼ cup oil and ½ cup of the brine.

MAYONNAISE

(Yield: approximately 3 cups)

5 *egg yolks*
1 *tablespoon mustard, half*
  French, half dry
½ *teaspoon of salt*
Pinch of cayenne pepper
½ *teaspoon Worcestershire*
sauce

¼ *cup of wine vinegar*
(lemon juice may be used
in place of vinegar)
1 *cup of olive oil*
1 *cup of good salad oil*

In a mixing bowl combine egg yolks, mustard, salt, pepper, Worcestershire sauce; beat well a few minutes, then add one third of vinegar. Beat in the oils, little at a time at first, and then in a gradually increasing quantity until oils are entirely used. Add remaining vinegar, beating well. Chill.

FLORIDA LOW-CALORIE FRENCH DRESSING

(Makes 1¼ cups)

1 *cup Florida grapefruit juice, divided*	½ *teaspoon paprika*
2 *teaspoons cornstarch*	½ *teaspoon dry mustard*
2 *tablespoons salad oil*	¼ *teaspoon Tabasco*
¾ *teaspoon salt*	¼ *cup catsup*
1 *teaspoon sugar*	1 *peeled clove garlic, minced* (optional)

Blend ½ cup grapefruit juice and cornstarch. Cook over low heat, stirring constantly, until thickened and clear. Remove from heat; add remaining ½ cup grapefruit juice. Measure remaining ingredients into small mixing bowl, add cornstarch mixture and beat with rotary beater until smooth. Store, covered, in refrigerator. Shake before using.

SPECIAL TARRAGON SALAD DRESSING

(Yield: approximately 2 cups)

4 *egg yolks*	*Few drops Worcestershire sauce*
¼ *cup fresh lemon juice*	
¼ *cup white wine*	1 *cup olive oil*
½ *teaspoon salt*	1 *tablespoon chopped tarragon (fresh, if available)*
½ *teaspoon English mustard*	
1 *pinch pepper*	
1 *pinch salt*	

Combine egg yolks, lemon juice, wine, and seasonings (except tarragon) in a mixing bowl. Beat for a few minutes with wire whisk. Add oil very slowly, a little at a time. Then add chopped tarragon.

Adjust seasoning to taste. If too sour, add a few tablespoons of water.

LONGCHAMPS SPECIAL SALAD DRESSING

(Yield: approximately 1 pint)

Garlic	½ teaspoon sugar
3 egg yolks	1 teaspoon salt
¼ cup wine vinegar, divided	Dash pepper
½ teaspoon paprika	1½ cups salad oil
½ teaspoon English mustard	¼ cup olive oil
½ teaspoon Worcestershire sauce	

Rub mixing bowl with ½ clove of garlic. Combine egg yolks with half the vinegar and all seasonings in a mixing bowl. Blend well. Stir in the salad and olive oil slowly with a wire whisk. Beat in remaining vinegar. Season to taste. Keep refrigerated.

YOGURT DRESSING

(Yield: 1 cup)

½ cup MAYONNAISE	⅛ tablespoon vegetable salt
½ cup yogurt	½ teaspoon lemon juice
¼ tablespoon honey	Rind ¼ lemon, grated

Beat all ingredients together. Serve with any raw-vegetable salad.

This dressing, which tastes like a sour-cream dressing, may also be varied by adding to it a few chopped olives or chopped water cress or finely chopped raw carrots.

FRENCH DRESSING (Serves 6)

1 *cup salad or olive oil*
¼ *cup wine vinegar*
Salt and pepper to taste

Mix well.

RUSSIAN DRESSING (Serves 6)

1 *cup* MAYONNAISE
¼ *cup chili sauce*
2 *tablespoons finely chopped sweet pickles*

1 *tablespoon red pepper*
1 *tablespoon green pepper*

Mix well.

ROQUEFORT DRESSING (Serves 6)

1 *cup* FRENCH DRESSING
¼ *cup mashed Roquefort cheese*

2 *tablespoons cream*
Pinch paprika

Mix well.

THOUSAND ISLAND DRESSING

(Serves 6)

1 *cup* MAYONNAISE
2 *tablespoons chili sauce*
2 *tablespoons finely chopped celery*
2 *tablespoons red pimento*

2 *tablespoons green pepper*
2 *tablespoons chopped hard-boiled egg*
½ *cup heavy cream*

Combine ingredients in a bowl and fold in stiffly beaten cream, unsweetened.

VINEGAR DRESSING

(Serves 6)

1 *cup* FRENCH DRESSING
1 *tablespoon chopped onions*
½ *tablespoon chopped*
parsley
½ *tablespoon chopped*
chives

1 *tablespoon chopped capers*
1 *tablespoon chopped*
hard-boiled egg

Mix well.

GREEN MAYONNAISE

(Yield: about 2 cups)

1½ *cups* MAYONNAISE
¼ *cup finely chopped*
parsley
¼ *cup finely chopped chives*

¼ *cup finely chopped water*
cress
Salt and pepper to taste

Combine all ingredients and blend well. Chill thoroughly.
This is an excellent sauce for any cold fish and for shellfish.

Sauces

In the kitchens of restaurants, hotels, and great houses the *saucier* ranks next to the head chef in status and in salary. Which is quite as it should be.

A good *saucier* is patient, sensitive, and imaginative. He watches a sauce every instant it is over the heat to see that, in spite of its heavy-bottomed pan, it does not scorch. With a wooden spoon or wire whisk he gently stirs, often or constantly. Above everything else he thoroughly blends the *roux* —butter and flour—so no harsh flour taste works through. Should a *saucier* add one or more egg yolks, depending, of course, upon the quantity of sauce being prepared, he will do this just before the sauce is completed, taking care to keep the heat low so the mixture never reaches a boil. Meticulously, he will control a sauce's consistency so it will become neither too thick nor too thin. He knows, by educated instinct, how much wine and seasoning are needed to accentuate, yet not mask, the true flavor of the food with which the sauce is to be served. Which means he will, conscientiously and often, use his tasting spoon.

None of this is intended to discourage anyone who wishes to add classic sauces to their repertoire. It is merely a roundabout way of saying that a cook must be ready to give sauce-making the not inconsiderable time and care that are its first essentials.

The recipes that follow have been chosen for two reasons: because they enjoy the greatest popularity and serve the widest variety of foods.

BASIC CREAM SAUCE

(Yield: 1 pint)

3 tablespoons butter
1½ tablespoons flour
2 cups milk
½ cup light cream
1 bay leaf
½ teaspoon salt
Dash white pepper

Melt butter in a saucepan. Mix in flour smoothly and cook over a low heat for several minutes. *Do not brown.* Add milk and cream. Cook, still over a low heat, stirring constantly, until sauce bubbles. Add bay leaf, salt, and pepper. Let bubble over a low heat for 15 to 20 minutes. Stir occasionally. Remove and discard bay leaf before using.

BASIC BROWN SAUCE

(Yield: 1 quart)

4 tablespoons shortening
4 pounds veal bones
2 onions, coarsely sliced
2 carrots, coarsely sliced
Few celery leaves, chopped
1 clove garlic, crushed
1 bay leaf
3 cloves
6 peppercorns, crushed

Pinch thyme
Pinch rosemary
1 tablespoon salt
4 tablespoons flour
1 can (10½ ounces) tomato
   purée
2 fresh tomatoes, chopped
2 quarts beef broth or water
⅓ cup sherry

Heat shortening in a large casserole or kettle, add bones and roast in a preheated 450° F (or hot) oven for 15 to 20 minutes or until well browned. Add onions, carrots, celery leaves, garlic, bay leaf, cloves, peppercorns, thyme, rosemary, and salt. Continue roasting 10 to 15 minutes longer. Stir in flour thoroughly and roast another 15 minutes.

Transfer to top of stove and add tomato purée, fresh tomatoes, broth or water. Bring to a boil, cover tightly, then reduce heat and simmer about 3 hours. Remove bones and discard. Strain liquid through a sieve, bring to a boil once again and skim off all fat. Stir in sherry and pour into glass jar and seal securely. Stores well under refrigeration for a week or so, or it can be frozen successfully.

HOLLANDAISE SAUCE

(Yield: 2 cups)

4 *egg yolks*
2 *tablespoons cream*
½ *pound* (2 *sticks*) *unsalted butter, melted*

Juice of 1 lemon
½ *teaspoon salt*
Dash cayenne

Stir egg yolks and cream together in the top of a double boiler. Use a wire whisk if you have one. Place over hot (not boiling) water and stir until mixture is thick as heavy cream.

Now add the hot melted butter very gradually, about 1 tablespoon at a time, and continue stirring constantly. Make sure water is hot, not boiling. When sauce is smooth and thick, remove from heat and add lemon juice, salt, and cayenne.

Hollandaise should be served warm, not hot. To keep warm, place container in a saucepan of *warm* water until ready to use.

BLENDER HOLLANDAISE

(Yield: ¾ cup)

½ cup (1 stick) butter	¼ teaspoon salt
3 egg yolks	Pinch cayenne
2 tablespoons lemon juice	

In a small saucepan heat butter to bubbling, but do not let it brown. Put egg yolks, lemon juice, salt, and cayenne in blender container. Cover container and turn motor on high. Immediately remove cover and quickly pour in the hot butter in a steady stream. When all the butter is added, turn motor off. Serve immediately or keep warm by placing the container in a saucepan containing *warm* water.

TOMATO SAUCE

(Yield: about 1 quart)

1 tablespoon shortening	Few sprigs parsley
1 carrot, sliced	Sprig fresh thyme or ¼
1 onion, sliced	teaspoon, dried
2 cloves garlic, crushed	1 bay leaf
Piece of ham bone (optional)	1½ teaspoons salt
1 tablespoon flour	¼ teaspoon pepper
6 large ripe tomatoes, cubed	1 teaspoon sugar
Few celery leaves	2 tablespoons butter

Melt shortening in a saucepan, add carrot, onion, garlic, and ham bone; cook over a low heat for about 10 minutes. Stir in flour as smoothly as possible and cook several minutes. Stir in the cubed tomatoes along with celery leaves, parsley, thyme, bay leaf, salt, pepper, and sugar. Bring to a boil; cover, reduce heat, and cook slowly until vegetables are very tender. Discard ham bone. Strain sauce through a fine sieve or blend in an electric blender. Stir in butter last of all.

BEARNAISE SAUCE

(Yield: 2 cups)

¼ cup tarragon vinegar
¼ cup dry white wine
6 peppercorns, crushed
Few sprigs tarragon or 1
   teaspoon, dried
4 egg yolks

1 tablespoon cream
½ pound (2 sticks) unsalted
   butter, melted
½ teaspoon salt
Dash cayenne

Combine vinegar, wine, peppercorns, and tarragon in the top of a double boiler. Cook over a brisk heat until liquid is reduced and mixture is almost dry. Set aside to cool.

When cold, stir in egg yolks and cream. Cook over hot, not boiling, water, stirring constantly until sauce looks creamy. Add hot melted butter gradually, a tablespoon at a time, and continue stirring constantly. Check to see that water is not boiling. Cook until smooth and thick. Season with salt and cayenne. Last of all, strain through a sieve.

Béarnaise Sauce is served warm, not hot. To keep it warm, place container of sauce in a pan of *warm* water.

MORNAY SAUCE

(Yield: about 1½ cups)

1 cup BASIC CREAM SAUCE
2 tablespoons grated
   Parmesan or Swiss cheese

2 egg yolks
2 tablespoons cream
2 tablespoons butter

Prepare 1 cup of Basic Cream Sauce. Remove from heat and stir in cheese. Beat egg yolks with cream, then stir in a spoonful or so of the hot sauce. Combine yolk mixture with sauce and heat, stirring constantly. *Do not boil.*

Stir in butter last of all.

SAUCE DIABLE

(Yield: about 1 cup)

¼ cup white wine
1 tablespoon prepared mustard
1 tablespoon chopped onion
1 can (7½-ounce size) brown gravy

Dash Worcestershire sauce
½ teaspoon salt
¼ teaspoon sugar

Cook white wine, mustard, and onion together until liquid has evaporated. Stir in brown gravy, cook to a boil, then simmer gently for 5 minutes. Work mixture through a sieve and season with Worcestershire sauce, salt, and sugar.

TARTAR SAUCE

(Yield: about 1½ cups)

1 cup MAYONNAISE
1 tablespoon finely chopped onions
2 tablespoons chopped pickles

1 teaspoon chopped capers
1 teaspoon chopped parsley
1 teaspoon German mustard
1 dash Worcestershire sauce

Blend well.

BORDELAISE SAUCE

(Yield: approximately 2 cups)

2 tablespoons of butter, divided
2 tablespoons of finely chopped shallots
1 cup of dry red wine
1½ cups of brown gravy

Salt and pepper to taste
½ cup sliced mushrooms, sautéed in a little butter
1 tablespoon of chopped parsley

Melt 1 tablespoon of the butter in a saucepan. Add the shallots and cook slowly for 5 minutes. Add the red wine and let simmer until reduced to about one third of the original quantity. Add the brown gravy, salt and pepper. Bring to a boil. Let cook a few minutes. Remove sauce from heat, add the mushrooms and chopped parsley; stir in the remaining butter.

REMOULADE SAUCE

(Yield: about 1½ cups)

1 cup MAYONNAISE
1 hard-boiled egg, chopped fine
1 teaspoon chopped parsley
½ teaspoon French mustard

1 teaspoon finely chopped tarragon
1 teaspoon anchovy paste
1 clove of garlic, puréed

Blend all ingredients well. Serve cold.

MADEIRA SAUCE

(Yield: about 1 cup)

1 tablespoon finely chopped shallots
1 tablespoon butter

¼ cup Madeira, divided
1 cup of brown gravy

Cook the peeled shallots in the butter for 4 to 5 minutes. Add half the Madeira wine and cook until the liquid is reduced to about 1 teaspoon. Add the brown gravy and let cook about 10 minutes. Strain. Add remaining Madeira just before serving. Serve hot.

CURRY SAUCE

(Yield: about 2 cups)

2 tablespoons of butter or shortening

1 large onion, minced

2 celery ribs, thinly sliced

2 cloves of garlic, crushed

Few sprigs of parsley

1 teaspoon of thyme

1 bay leaf

2 tablespoons of flour

3 tablespoons of curry powder

2 tablespoons of shredded coconut

1 green apple, cored and sliced

1 tablespoon of tomato purée

Salt and pinch of sugar, to taste

2 cups of chicken broth or water

Melt the butter or shortening in a casserole. Add onions, celery, garlic, parsley sprigs, thyme, and bay leaf. Let simmer slowly until slightly browned. Add the flour and mix well. Add the curry powder, coconut, apple, tomato purée, salt, and sugar. Blend thoroughly. Add the chicken broth or water. Bring to a boil and cook slowly for 1 hour. Strain. Bring to boil once more.

Note: If a mild sauce is desired, add a few tablespoons of cream and some finely chopped chutney.

AND DESSERT SAUCES . . .

MELBA SAUCE

(Serves 6)

*½ pound fresh raspberries or 1½ containers frozen
raspberries*
8 ounces currant jelly

If fresh raspberries are used, wash carefully. Force raspberries, fresh or frozen and thawed, through a fine sieve with the currant jelly. Blend well with a wire whip and serve very cold.

CHOCOLATE SAUCE

(Yield: about 2½ cups)

*½ pound of unsweetened
chocolate squares*
1 cup light cream
1½ cups sugar

Pinch of salt
3 tablespoons butter
1 teaspoon vanilla extract

In a small saucepan combine chocolate with cream and cook over low heat, stirring until chocolate is melted. Add sugar and salt, stirring until sugar is melted and mixture has thickened—about 5 minutes. Stir in the butter and vanilla; remove from fire. Serve warm.

HARD SAUCE

A hard sauce, which serves many hot desserts—such as puddings, apple charlotte, mince pie, APPLE STRUDEL—is an uncooked sauce made of sugar and butter with whatever additional flavoring is desired. The sauce, which should be chilled, melts over the warm dessert in a slow trickle.

Use three parts of sugar to one part of butter. First, cream the butter, then add the sugar gradually. The longer these ingredients are blended the creamier the sauce will be.

It is effective to shape this sauce into rosettes, using a pastry bag to form the rosettes on waxed paper. Then chill. Later, remove rosettes from waxed paper and use to decorate dessert they are to serve.

BRANDY HARD SAUCE

Cream ½ cup sweet butter and gradually beat in 1½ cups of granulated sugar, 4 tablespoons of good brandy, and a pinch of nutmeg.

CHOCOLATE HARD SAUCE

Cream ½ cup sweet butter with 1½ cups of granulated sugar and 4 tablespoons of grated unsweetened chocolate. Alternate in adding the sugar and chocolate.

FRENCH HARD SAUCE

Cream ½ cup sweet butter. Gradually beat in 1½ cups of granulated sugar, 1 tablespoon brandy, 1 tablespoon Benedictine, and 1 tablespoon Chartreuse. Alternate in adding the sugar, brandy, Benedictine, and Chartreuse. Add a pinch of nutmeg.

KIRSCH-ALMOND HARD SAUCE

Cream ½ cup sweet butter, then gradually beat in 1½ cups of granulated sugar. While beating butter and sugar together, add 2 tablespoons of kirsch and 3 tablespoons of ground, toasted almonds.

BUTTERSCOTCH SAUCE

(Yield: about 1½ cups)

1 *cup brown sugar*	1 *tablespoon butter*
¼ *cup light cream*	*Pinch salt*
½ *cup corn syrup*	*Vanilla*

Combine all ingredients, with the exception of the vanilla, in a saucepan and bring to a boil over low heat. Let cook for 10 minutes, stirring occasionally. Remove from heat and add vanilla. Serve warm.

CHERRY SAUCE

1 *can (size no. 2½) black*	1 *tablespoon of cornstarch*
cherries (Please see note)	2 *tablespoons kirsch or any*
1 *tablespoon of sugar*	*other liqueur*

Drain cherries and reserve juice. Combine sugar, cornstarch, and liqueur. Bring the drained juice to a boil in a saucepan. Stir cornstarch mixture, slowly, into the boiling juice, until thickened. Reduce heat, add the cherries, blend well and let cook 5 to 10 minutes, until cherries are heated thoroughly. Serve with slightly sugared whipped cream (optional).

STRAWBERRY SAUCE

1 *quart fresh strawberries*   ¼ *cup* MELBA SAUCE
½ *cup granulated sugar*
2 *tablespoons Grand*
   Marnier or any other
   liqueur

Clean and wash berries, then place them in a bowl and crush or cut very fine. Mix in sugar, liqueur, and Melba Sauce and let stand 20 to 30 minutes, covered. Serve with slightly sugared whipped cream (optional).

Note: Both Cherry and Strawberry sauces can also be used as an accompaniment for ice creams, puddings, custards, or French pancakes.

Sandwiches

The sandwich is reputed to have originated with John Montagu, an inveterate gambler, who chose to have his meat and, sometimes, his vegetables served between slices of bread so that he might dine at the gaming table. There can be no question that the sandwich was named for him, for he was the fourth Earl of Sandwich. But it did not originate with him. Many, many years before the earl's time those who worked on farms and those who went traveling found it convenient to carry their meat, fish, poultry, eggs, vegetables, or cheese between slices of bread.

There are all kinds of sandwiches: the dainty assorted sandwiches of the tearoom, the superman heros of the deli, and the haphazard—and sometimes surprisingly tasty—sandwiches which, for practical reasons, combine anything found on the cupboard or refrigerator shelf.

There also are special sandwiches—hot or cold, open or closed—concocted as carefully as any other good food. It is not, for instance, by chance that the bread of a Longchamps cold roast-beef sandwich is a cross between pumpernickel and rye bread. Or that the base of an oyster club sandwich, which receives a mere flick of Tabasco and cayenne and a touch of fresh horse-radish, is a hot, toasted roll. Or that, in the sandwich suggestions that follow, different spreads, breads, and garnishings are recommended.

WHEN YOU MAKE SANDWICHES

Sandwich bread, toast, or split rolls may be spread with butter, cottage cheese, creamed butter, or cream cheese. Always, however, have the spread soft enough to handle easily.

If toast is used, butter it immediately it is done. The butter will preserve the moisture, keep the bread from drying too quickly.

A sandwich's filling should extend to all four corners of the bread, so that no bite will be disappointingly dry.

Top the filling with a crisp lettuce leaf, water cress, or other green.

Trim the completed sandwiches neatly so neither filling nor green overlap the bread.

Whether or not the crust, too, is trimmed is a matter of personal preference.

SUGGESTIONS FOR GARNISHINGS

The garnishing of a sandwich is important. Not only does it add to the sandwich's eye appeal, it also offers a complementary flavor. A few suggestions:

Dill pickles, sliced, cut in fan shape or sticks, served with tomato slices in a lettuce leaf.

Coleslaw, sprigs of water cress, shredded lettuce, or crisp lettuce leaves filled with HORSE-RADISH or MAYONNAISE, RUSSIAN DRESSING or TARTAR SAUCE; olives, black or green, ripe or stuffed or pitted, and filled with cottage cheese or red pimento.

Radishes, shaped like roses.

Relishes: tomato and onion, pickled beets, chowchow, pickled cauliflower, pickled cucumbers.

SANDWICHES

The fillings for sandwiches are as limitless as your imagination. Longchamps favorites, in addition to those mentioned in the introduction to this chapter are:

CAPE COD SANDWICH

On a slice of hot buttered toast place a generous layer of creamed, flaked crabmeat, not too moist. Top this with slices of American cheese and set under the broiler until the cheese is thoroughly melted. Cover with another piece of hot buttered toast and serve immediately. Garnish with a lettuce leaf holding sticks of sweet pickle.

SMOKED SALMON AND CREAM CHEESE ON RYE

Spread, generously, a slice of rye bread with cream cheese. Arrange slices of smoked salmon on the cream cheese. Top with a second slice of rye, also generously spread with cream cheese. Cut in half, thirds, or quarters. Garnish with a lettuce leaf filled with slices of raw onion and ripe olives.

COMBINATION ON RYE

Spread a slice of rye bread with butter and mustard. English or French mustard is especially desirable. Arrange thin slices of Swiss cheese, cooked smoked ham, and chicken on the bread; top with crisp lettuce. Cover with a second slice of rye bread spread with butter and mustard. Cut in half or fours. Decorate with coleslaw in a lettuce leaf, tomato slices, and dill pickle.

BACON, CHICKEN, AND ANCHOVIES ON TOAST

On a slice of the bread of your choice, buttered and mayonnaised, place broiled bacon. Top this with lettuce leaf. Place sliced chicken on top of the lettuce. And place anchovy filets on top of the chicken. Cover with a second slice of buttered and mayonnaised bread. Garnish with sliced tomatoes on a lettuce leaf.

CREAM CHEESE AND ALMOND

(Yield: 2 sandwiches)

Spread slices of whole-wheat, raisin, nut, or any fruit bread with a mixture of:

2 *tablespoons cream cheese*   *Salt, pepper, and paprika to*
1 *tablespoon pickle relish*   *taste*
1 *tablespoon ground almonds*   *Dash Worcestershire sauce*
2 *tablespoons finely chopped*
celery

Garnish with water cress and radish roses.

BACON AND TOMATO

Broil 4 slices of bacon for each sandwich. Place the bacon with tomato slices and crisp lettuce leaves between slices of buttered, mayonnaised toast. Cheesebread, toasted, is recommended. Serve with coleslaw and dill pickle.

CLUB SANDWICH

(Serves 1)

3 *slices freshly made toast*   3 *slices of chicken*
4 *small crisp leaves of lettuce*   3 *slices of crisp bacon*
2 *teaspoons of mayonnaise*   3 *slices of tomato*

Butter the toast. On one slice place 2 lettuce leaves, 1 teaspoon mayonnaise, and 3 slices of chicken. Place a slice of toast on top of this and arrange on it 2 lettuce leaves, 3 slices of bacon, 3 tomato slices, and 1 teaspoon mayonnaise. Cover with third slice of toast. Press down lightly and cut in quarters. Secure each quarter with a frilled toothpick. Garnish with pickles, olives, radishes, and a few potato chips.

WESTERN SANDWICH

(Serves 1)

2 *eggs, slightly beaten*   1 *tablespoon chopped,*
1 *teaspoon finely chopped*   *cooked green pepper*
   onions, sautéed in butter
1 *tablespoon finely diced*
   ham

Mix the above ingredients thoroughly. Fry on both sides. Serve between two slices of freshly made, buttered toast. Garnish with sliced tomato and pimento-stuffed olives.

Desserts

Desserts are not what they used to be. In this diet-conscious age few would allow themselves the *pâtisseries* that once adorned banquet tables. They were filled, frequently, those *pâtisseries*, with a rich, coffee-flavored custard. They were festooned with garlands of sugared violets and rose petals, marrons, nutmeats, and angelica. They were fluted with whipped cream. And they were bordered with candied fruits and spun sugar. It was for such sumptuous "mounted pieces"—in the form of fountains, Roman ruins, and other architectural displays—that Carême, "the chef of kings and the king of chefs" won his fame.

It is just as well we no longer would favor any such extravaganzas. The days of painstaking care that would go into their preparation would make them prohibitive.

However, we bend too far toward austerity, I think, when, ruefully, we refuse sauces or whipped cream and, sorrowfully, shake our heads over marzipan or even little iced cakes while, with horror, we count their calories.

I do not favor any dessert being modified until it is comparatively nonfattening. For it then is not likely to be worth the calories it still contains. Better, I say, to have a dessert as the chef who originated it intended it to be and be served only a little of it. A COUPE SUTHERLAND, for instance, should never be denied its wine-flavored ZABAGLIONE SAUCE. Nor should any strudel or cobbler come to the table without a creamy hard sauce, preferably one that has been laced with brandy.

Only one of the recipes that follow—ORANGE SURPRISE, BONNE AUBERGE—is for a delicious sweet, low in calories.

When I was a small boy in Scandinavia, I learned a saying I have never forgotten, it reflects such a joy of living: "If it's going to be Christmas, let it be Christmas!" I'll paraphrase it, if I may, to say "If it's going to be a dessert, let it be a dessert"—however small the portion!

CREME BRULEE

(Serves 5 to 6)

3 *cups heavy cream*   1 *tablespoon vanilla extract*
⅓ *cup granulated sugar*   ⅓ *cup light brown sugar*
7 *egg yolks*

Heat the cream and the granulated sugar in a double boiler. Stir once or twice so the sugar dissolves. Do not let it boil. Beat the egg yolks with a wire whisk. Pour the hot cream over the beaten yolks, little by little, while stirring vigorously. Add the vanilla. Strain the mixture into a baking dish. Set the dish in a pan of hot water, with the water safely below the dish side. Bake in a preheated oven of 300° F for 30 minutes or until a silver knife inserted in the crème comes out clean. Remove from oven and let cool thoroughly. Before serving, sprinkle brown sugar evenly over the crème's surface. Then place under the broiler until the sugar is melted and caramelized. It is advisable to stand by during this process so the crème can be turned any time it is about to scorch at any spot. Serve immediately or chill and serve cold. A sauce of crushed strawberries, served separately, is a perfect complement to a Crème Brûlée.

STRAWBERRIES ROMANOFF

(Serves 6)

1 *quart of fresh strawberries*   3 *cups of lightly sweetened*
4 *ounces of Grand Marnier*   *whipped cream*
4 *tablespoons of sugar*   4 *scoops of vanilla ice cream*
Rind of 2 oranges, grated
2 *tablespoons of* MELBA
  SAUCE

Wash strawberries and remove stems. Place in a bowl. Add Grand Marnier, sugar, orange rind, and Melba Sauce. Toss a few times to blend. Cover with a plate and chill in refrigerator for 1 hour. Remove berries from the refrigerator. Add the whipped cream; mix. Then add the ice cream and stir just enough to blend all the ingredients.

Divide the mixture into individual sherbet glasses or a deep dessert dish. Serve immediately.

STRAWBERRIES JUBILEE

(Serves 6)

½ cup of water   4 ounces of kirsch
½ cup of sugar   6 scoops of vanilla ice cream
1 tablespoon of cornstarch
1 quart of strawberries, stems
   removed, washed

Bring the water and sugar to a boil. Mix the cornstarch with a little water and add, stirring, to the boiling water-sugar mixture. Add the strawberries. Bring to a boil and let cook 4 to 5 minutes. Add the kirsch and ignite. Serve at once as flaming sauce over the ice cream.

FRESH STRAWBERRY TART

(Serves 6 to 8)

PASTRY:

2 cups sifted all-purpose   1 cup softened butter
   flour   1 tablespoon sugar
¼ teaspoon salt   Grated rind of 1 lemon
2 egg yolks

FILLING:

1 pint heavy cream   SPONGECAKE
4 to 6 tablespoons   1 quart strawberries
   confectioners' sugar   6 tablespoons strawberry
1 teaspoon vanilla   jam

Make pastry first. Sift flour and salt into a bowl. Scoop out a hollow in center of flour and drop in unbeaten egg yolks, butter, sugar, lemon rind. Mix together with your hands to make a thick paste. Transfer to a 10-inch rectangle cake pan and pat an even layer over bottom and around sides. Prick with fork tines and refrigerate until firm. Bake in a pre-heated 425° F (or hot) oven for 10 to 15 minutes or until pastry is golden brown. Cool.

To assemble the tart: Whip the cream until it holds a soft shape. Stir in confectioners' sugar and vanilla. Spoon into pastry shell and cover with thin slices of Spongecake. Cover the cake with hulled strawberries. Heat strawberry jam until it spreads easily, then work the jam through a sieve to remove seeds. Spread evenly over berries to give a professional glaze. Chill well before serving.

SPONGECAKE

1 *cup sifted cake flour*
2 *teaspoons baking powder*
¼ *teaspoon salt*
3 *eggs*
1 *cup sugar*

¼ *cup boiling water*
1 *tablespoon lemon juice*
1 *teaspoon grated lemon rind*

Sift together flour, baking powder, and salt. Separate egg yolks from whites and beat yolks very hard until light in color. Add sugar gradually and continue beating vigorously until mixture looks fluffy. Beat in boiling water, lemon juice, and lemon rind. Add sifted dry ingredients gradually and beat until batter is well blended.

Beat egg whites until they hold a point when egg beater is lifted. Add to batter and fold in gently but thoroughly. Pour into an ungreased 9-inch tube pan and bake in a pre-heated 325° F (or slow) oven for about 50 minutes. Invert pan to cool. Remove cake when cold.

COUPE SUTHERLAND

(Serves 6)

Zabaglione:

12 *egg yolks*	3 *tablespoons sugar*
⅓ *cup Marsala wine*	*Grated rind of 1 lemon*
⅓ *cup sherry*	*Grated rind of 1 orange*

6 MERINGUE SHELLS
1 *pint raspberry sherbet*
Chopped pistachio nuts

Place egg yolks, Marsala wine, sherry, sugar, lemon and orange rinds in top of double boiler over hot, not boiling, water. Beat steadily with a wire whisk until mixture thickens. You must be watchful here because Zabaglione will curdle if overcooked.

Immediately the Zabaglione is custardlike, cool over ice or in refrigerator.

To serve: place Meringue Shells on serving plates, fill each with a big scoop of raspberry sherbet, spoon a generous serving of Zabaglione over each, and sprinkle tops with chopped pistachio nuts.

ORANGE SURPRISE BONNE AUBERGE

(Serves 4)

4 *large, firm oranges*
1 *cup* MACEDOINE OF FRUIT
4 *scoops of lemon, raspberry, orange, or pineapple*
    sherbet or ice
4 *sprigs fresh mint*

Macédoine of Fruit:

- 1 *cup equal parts of any fresh fruit, sliced, diced, or cut in sticks*
- 1 *tablespoon sugar*
- 2 *ounces of liqueur, preferably kirsch or Grand Marnier*

Combine the ingredients of the Macédoine in a bowl, cover and chill for 1 to 2 hours.

Cut ½ inch from the tops of the oranges. Cut ⅛ inch from the bottom so oranges will stand firmly. Scoop out pulp and pits. Just before serving divide the Macédoine of Fruit evenly in the orange shells and top with scoop of chosen sherbet or ice. Add a sprig of fresh mint for flavor and attractiveness.

SOUFFLE GRAND MARNIER

(Serves 5 to 6)

3 *tablespoons butter*	¼ *cup sugar*
4 *tablespoons flour*	¼ *cup Grand Marnier*
¾ *cup milk*	2 *additional egg whites*
4 *whole eggs, separated*	

Melt butter in a saucepan, then stir in flour smoothly and cook for a minute or two. Pour in milk and cook over a low heat, stirring constantly, until sauce is smooth and bubbly. Cool slightly.

Beat egg yolks until light in color, then stir in the sugar. Blend in the warm sauce thoroughly, following with the Grand Marnier. Beat the 6 egg whites until they hold a definite point when you lift up the beater. Fold into the yolk mixture very gently. Pour into a buttered, lightly sugared soufflé dish or straight-sided casserole (1½-quart size) and bake in a preheated 375° F (or moderate) oven for 30 to

35 minutes or until soufflé has puffed and browned. Serve immediately.

Note: For a delicious sauce, crush 1 pint of fresh strawberries, then stir in 2 tablespoons of sugar and 4 tablespoons of Grand Marnier.

APPLE STRUDEL

(Serves 6 to 8)

½ pound soft butter, divided   *1 cup sugar*
4 eggs   *1 teaspoon cinnamon*
2 cups all-purpose flour   *Grated rind of 2 lemons*
½ teaspoon salt   *½ cup raisins or currants*
8 greening apples, medium   *½ cup chopped almonds*
size

Beat half the butter (¼ pound or 1 stick) with the eggs vigorously, then gradually mix in flour and salt. Use your hand and work or beat the dough for 15 minutes at least. During this beating you will see the dough change from a sticky consistency to a ball of soft dough that pulls away from the bowl. Cover with an inverted bowl while you prepare the filling.

Pare, core, and cut apples into thin slices. Mix with sugar, cinnamon, lemon rind, raisins or currants, and chopped almonds. Melt remaining ¼ pound of butter.

Spread a clean cloth over a large table. Sprinkle cloth with a generous coating of flour, put ball of dough in center and roll with a rolling pin into a large even circle. Now, with a gentle hand-over-hand motion, work or stretch dough from center to the outer edge. Be careful not to tear. When dough is as thin as tissue paper, trim off thick uneven edges to make a neat rectangle. Spread apple mixture over half the dough and sprinkle with 2 tablespoons of melted butter. Roll neatly, starting with the apple-covered side, pushing the roll along with the cloth. Tuck in the ends neatly and place on a greased pan. Brush top with melted butter and bake in a preheated 400° F (or moderately hot) oven for 30 minutes. Reduce heat to 350°F (or moderate) and continue baking 10 to 15 minutes longer or until handsomely browned. Sprinkle with confectioners' sugar and serve warm with lightly sweetened cream or HARD SAUCE.

FRUIT-RUM CAKE

(Yield: 4 small loaves)

¼ cup diced candied fruit	½ pound unsweetened
¼ cup raisins	butter
¼ cup rum	½ teaspoon vanilla
1 cup all-purpose flour	1 cup sugar
1 tablespoon baking powder	4 eggs
Pinch salt	

Combine candied fruit, raisins, and rum in a bowl. Cover and let stand for several hours. Sift together flour, baking powder, and salt. Set aside. Work or cream butter and vanilla together until soft. Gradually work in sugar until mixture is extremely light and creamy. Use an electric mixer, if you have one. Beat in the eggs, 2 at a time, alternately with flour mixture. Beat hard after each addition. Stir in fruit-rum combination last of all. Pour into 4 greased loaf pans (8× 4×3 inches) and bake in a preheated 350° F (or moderate) oven for 10 minutes. At this point pull them out of the oven and make an incision lengthwise in the center of each cake with a small knife. Return cakes to oven and continue baking 40 to 50 minutes longer or until cakes pull away from sides of pan. Cool on rack for about 10 minutes, then turn out and cool completely.

Fruit-Rum Cakes keep extremely well if wrapped in foil and refrigerated.

FLOATING ISLAND

(Serves 4 to 5)

2½ cups of milk
½ cup granulated sugar
1 teaspoon of vanilla extract
6 egg whites

¾ cup powdered sugar
6 egg yolks
2 tablespoons of toasted
  sliced almonds

Put the milk, granulated sugar, and vanilla in a shallow saucepan. Bring to a boil, stirring well to melt sugar.

Meanwhile, beat the egg whites until foamy. Then, gradually, add the powdered sugar, continuing to beat until the egg whites are stiff. Scoop up this meringue, spoonful by spoonful and drop into the slowly boiling milk. Turn each meringue carefully after about one minute, using a skimmer or two forks. After the meringues have cooked for an additional two minutes, remove them from the milk, using a perforated spoon. Place meringues on a dry cloth to drain.

To make the cream pudding:

Strain the milk in which the meringues have cooked. Beat the egg yolks. Gradually add the strained milk to them. Return to the fire and stir until the mixture begins to thicken. *Do not let boil.* Remove from the fire to cool. When quite cold put the cream pudding in a shallow dessert dish or bowl and arrange the poached meringues on top. Sprinkle with toasted sliced almonds.

MERINGUES CHANTILLY

(Yield: 15 to 18 shells)

MERINGUE SHELLS:

6 egg whites
Pinch salt
1½ cups confectioners' sugar

Grease a cookie sheet and coat lightly with flour. Beat egg whites and salt together until mixture begins to hold a shape. Add sugar, a little at a time, beating constantly, until the whites hold a definite point when you lift up the beater.

Shape little oval mounds (about 4 inches long) with 2 spoons or a pastry bag fitted with a round tube. Keep meringues about 1 inch apart on the cookie sheet. Bake in a preheated 200°F oven for 1 to 1¼ hours or until light gold in color and almost firm on tops.

Remove from the cookie sheet immediately with a broad spatula. Press the slightly soft undersides with the back of a teaspoon to make oval-shaped hollows. Cool on a rack. (Do not attempt to make these on a hot, humid day.)

Filling for Meringues Chantilly:

Fill the Meringue Shells with whipped cream, flavored with sugar and vanilla, and top with a second shell.

VANILLA CUSTARD PUDDING

(Serves 6)

1 *pint half-and-half (milk and cream)*	3 *whole eggs*
	1 *egg yolk*
¼ *cup sugar*	*Pinch salt*
½ *teaspoon vanilla extract*	

Heat milk and cream over low heat until a film shines on top. Meanwhile, mix sugar, vanilla extract, whole eggs, egg yolk, and salt together in a bowl. Add the hot milk gradually, stirring constantly, until sugar has dissolved. Pour into 6 custard cups. Place cups in a pan of hot, not boiling, water and bake in a 350° F (or moderate) oven for 20 to 25 minutes or until a knife inserted in the center comes out clean. Cool.

When cold, run the blade of a small knife around the edge

of each custard to loosen the custard and invert on a dessert plate.

Serve with BUTTERSCOTCH SAUCE, MELBA SAUCE or CHOCOLATE SAUCE, whipped cream, or a garnish of fresh fruits.

PEACHES WITH VANILLA ICE CREAM AND MELBA SAUCE [Peach Melba]

(Serves 6)

3 *fresh peaches or 6 canned peach halves*
2 *tablespoons granulated sugar*
2 *tablespoons water*
½ *teaspoon vanilla*

1 *pint vanilla ice cream*
6 *tablespoons toasted sliced almonds*
MELBA SAUCE
½ *pint cream*

If fresh peaches are used, choose ripe ones. To loosen skins, dip them into boiling water for about 4 minutes. Peel. Cook in sugar syrup of half water and half sugar and vanilla for 5 minutes, or until tender. Do not overcook. Chill in syrup. If fresh peaches are used, cut in half. Put vanilla ice cream in individual glass dishes, top it with half a peach, round side up. Pour one tablespoon Melba Sauce over each, sprinkle with toasted sliced almonds. Garnish with lightly sugared whipped cream.

PEARS WITH CHOCOLATE SAUCE AND WHIPPED CREAM [Poire Belle Hélène]

Follow the same procedure as for Peach Melba, substituting pears for the peaches and using CHOCOLATE SAUCE instead of MELBA SAUCE.

PUFF PASTRIES WITH CREAM FILLING [Pâte à Chou]

(Yield: 16 to 18 puffs)

Cream Puffs:

1 cup water	1 cup all-purpose flour
½ cup unsalted butter	4 eggs
Pinch salt	

Combine water, butter, and salt in a saucepan. Bring to a boil, then remove from heat and stir in the flour all at once. Return pan to heat and beat with a wooden spoon for several minutes or until dough leaves the sides of the pan and forms a mass. Remove from heat and beat in eggs, one at a time. Beat smooth after each addition.

Using a tablespoon or pastry bag with tip, shape small puffs on a greased cookie sheet. Bake in a preheated 375° F (or moderate) oven for 15 to 20 minutes or until puffs are golden brown. Remove from cookie sheet and cool.

Cream Filling:

2 cups milk	6 tablespoons flour
6 egg yolks	Dash salt
⅓ cup sugar	1 teaspoon vanilla

Heat milk in a saucepan until a film shines on the surface. In the top of a double boiler combine egg yolks, sugar, flour, salt. Stir in hot milk very gradually. Cook over boiling water, stirring constantly, until smooth and thick. Flavor with vanilla, melted chocolate, coffee essence or powdered instant coffee, or any desired liqueur. Cool.

Slit tops off little Cream Puffs with a sharp knife. Fill centers with Cream Filling and replace tops. Serve cold with CHOCOLATE SAUCE.

RICE PUDDING WITH RAISINS

¾ cup rice
3 cups water
1 quart milk
¾ cup sugar
¼ teaspoon salt
½ cup raisins

4 egg yolks
1 cup heavy cream, divided
1 teaspoon vanilla
Grated rind of 1 lemon
Powdered cinnamon

Wash rice in several waters, drain, then add 3 cups boiling water and cook for 10 minutes. In other words, parboil. Drain off water and combine rice, milk, sugar, and salt; cook over a moderate heat for 25 to 30 minutes or until rice is tender and mixture is thick. Cook raisins in a little boiling water for about 10 minutes. Drain.

Beat egg yolks in a separate bowl with half the cream. Add to rice mixture along with raisins, vanilla, and lemon rind. Transfer to a casserole, spread a thin layer of cream, whipped until stiff, on top and sprinkle with cinnamon. Bake in a preheated 400° F (or moderately hot) oven for about 8 minutes or until cream turns golden. Cool and serve just as it is or with more cream.

BREAD-AND-BUTTER PUDDING

(Serves 6)

12 slices French bread or 6
   slices white bread, cut in
   half
⅓ cup butter
½ cup raisins
3 cups milk

4 eggs
½ cup sugar
¼ teaspoon salt
1 teaspoon vanilla
Confectioners' sugar

Toast French or white bread and spread with butter. Arrange slices in bottom of a large shallow baking dish (butter the dish generously) and sprinkle with raisins. Set aside.

Heat milk until a film shines on the surface. Beat eggs, sugar, salt, and vanilla in a bowl, then gradually stir in the hot milk. Pour mixture over bread slices and let stand about 15 minutes. Place baking dish in a pan containing 1 inch of hot water and bake in a preheated 350° F (or moderate) oven for 45 to 50 minutes. Sprinkle top with confectioners' sugar and serve warm.

FRENCH PANCAKES

(Yield: about 24 cakes)

2 *cups all-purpose flour*	6 *eggs*
½ *teaspoon salt*	2 *cups milk*

Sift flour and salt together in a bowl. In a separate bowl beat eggs vigorously. Then beat in the milk. Combine the dry ingredients, using as few strokes as possible. Ignore the lumps—they will take care of themselves.

Heat and grease a 5-inch skillet. The skillet will be the right temperature when several drops of cold water tested on it dance about. Add a small amount of batter, tipping the skillet so that batter will cover the bottom of the pan, thinly. Cook over medium heat until nicely browned. Turn and brown the second side. Roll if desired. Serve with MELBA SAUCE, CHERRY SAUCE, or STRAWBERRY SAUCE.

RUM OMELETTE FLAMBE

(Serves 2)

6 *eggs*	1 *tablespoon butter*
2 *tablespoons sugar*	*Confectioners' sugar*
Pinch salt	5 *tablespoons rum*

Combine eggs, sugar, salt in a mixing bowl and beat thoroughly. Heat butter in a 10-inch omelette pan (or skillet with sloping sides) until bubbly hot but not brown. Use a moderate heat. Pour in egg mixture and stir with a fork until omelette begins to "set." Run the fork around the sides to prevent sticking. When lightly browned on the bottom and almost firm, fold omelette in half with a broad spatula and turn upside down on a heated platter. Sprinkle generously with confectioners' sugar. Pour heated rum over surface and ignite with a match. Baste omelette with the flaming rum until sugar is delicately browned. Serve immediately.

Good Wine—
No Nonsense

Often, talking or reading about wine, I am reminded of an Englishwoman who sat across the dining room from me at a hotel on Tangier Bay, in North Africa. She was a remittance woman. As long as she stayed out of England her husband paid her an income considerably in excess of what the British law would have required of him. She had no wealth. But she could afford to live pleasantly. In the heat of the day she could play bridge for ladylike stakes in the hotel's cool, tiled lounge. Evenings, she could buy little stacks of chips at the casino. And she always had a bottle of wine on her table.

I can see her, still, marking the wine line on her bottle to insure against it being enjoyed in the pantry. She relished her wine; never a great wine but a fresh *vin ordinaire*. If her waiter was slow to bring a wineglass she would spill the water from her goblet back into the pitcher and drink her wine from her goblet. As she drank, a faint flush would come to her high-boned cheeks, the corners of her mouth would soften, a little light would be kindled in her eyes and I would see, sitting in her place, the woman she had been when she was young and, undoubtedly, lovely.

It is the beauty of wine that, whatever our circumstances or our age, it awakens our happier self.

The poets have sung of wine always. For thousands of years it has gladdened hearts and benefited appetites and digestion. It contains many healthy things: fruit sugars, B vitamins, minerals, and, in addition, certain blessed qualities that retard the way its low alcoholic content (something between 10 per cent and 20 per cent, usually) enters our systems. Wine also is a tranquilizer. In the countries where wine—considered as necessary as bread or meat—appears on all tables, the sale of tranquilizers is negligible.

We find wine appearing in the hieroglyphics of the ancients. The Bible, in both the Old and the New Testaments, has praise for it; some criticism too. The early Greeks, who learned from the Egyptians how to ferment the grape's juice, drank their wine with great pleasure and exported it to the Romans with great profit. Ever since the beginning of the fifteenth century the story of wine has been woven into tapestries; one of which shows a rabbit and a fox sprouting wings as they sniff a wine. Some scholars believe that the word wine derives not from the vine but from *vis*, the Latin for strength. Significantly, during unhappy periods in history the production of wine has always fallen off.

It was to encourage the appreciation of wine—the lamentable underrated American wines, especially—that led to Longchamps' complimentary service of wine at dinner. I, a businessman—with personal tastes as expensive as the financing of Broadway plays and the collecting of works of modern artists—value the rich revenue of the bar. But I am not so avaricious that I do not prefer to see my patrons drink wine with their dinner rather than another cocktail or highball. Spirits dull the palate. Wine woos food's flavor. And I take pride in the Longchamps kitchens.

There are fewer calories in wine. A 2½-ounce martini has 180 calories, a rum and cola or a 3½-ounce whisky sour has 225 calories, and a 2½-ounce manhattan has 250 calories. An 8-ounce bottle of beer has 110 calories. Scotch, bourbon, and rye are computed to contain 100 calories to the ounce, gin 125 calories to 1½ ounces, and rum 150 calories to 1½ ounces. But there are only 100 calories in 4 ounces of dry champagne or 3½ ounces of dry sherry, and only 80 calories in 4 ounces of a dry table wine.

It is unfortunate that the nonsense of the wine snobs should inhibit anyone—and it is my personal conviction that it inhibits many—from enjoying the pleasant accompaniment that wine is to dining.

There is, the esoterics would have us believe, only one way

to wrap a napkin around a bottle, to carry wine in a basket, or pour it from a basket. Other absurdities perpetuate the idea that wine, to be good, must be expensive, imported, and old. There is endless foolishness, too, about what wine goes with what, the need for a different glass for every wine, the precise temperature at which different wines should be served, and the impropriety of smoking when drinking wine.

The manner in which a napkin is wrapped around a bottle is unimportant provided the napkin is fresh and the fold tidy. Actually a napkin is not necessary.

Originally, a napkin was used to guard against the very, very slight chance that injury might result from a bottle breaking while being decorked. Today we have excellent corkscrews with good true worms. Also fewer and fewer bottles require decorking. Many bottles are now fitted with plastic stoppers and caps such as are used on bottles of beer. A napkin also was used to catch the icy drips from a bottle that had been cooled in a bucket. Today, except in restaurants, buckets are rarely used. Electrical refrigerators chill wine to perfection.

Wine that is fitted with plastic stoppers or caps does not even need to be stored on its side, there being no necessity for keeping a cork moist so it will not shrink and admit air, which spoils wine.

The need for a wine basket is disappearing too; unless a wine is a great wine that has been brought to considerable age. Both American and European vintners have, in the last several years, largely learned to avoid sedimentation. And the purpose of a basket was to keep any sediment on the bottom side of the bottle where it would remain, if gently handled, even as the wine was poured.

Wine is a luxury only when we choose to make it so. An excellent fifth of red or white table wine—which is equal to eight glasses—can be bought for $1.50. And there are good wines that sell for even less.

Most wines should be drunk as soon as they mature or when they are about one year old.

Do not let me seem to deny the superiority of great wines: the result of grapes being blended into a perfect mixture, of the wine being drawn from the vat at the exact moment when fermentation has quieted, of bottles being stored—with tender, loving care—long enough but not too long.

Currently, great wines are not notable in the United States. But they will be. Meanwhile we have many excellent wines. And the wider patronage we give these wines the thinner the vintners will be able to spread their overhead and the less these wines will cost.

We do well to remember our third president, Thomas Jefferson, one of those rare men who made it a life-long habit to be appreciative and wise. He told us: "No nation is drunken where wine is cheap; and none sober where the dearness of wine substitutes ardent spirits as the common beverage."

The Prohibition Era of 1919 to 1933, which resulted in a deplorable falling off in the quality of United States wines, undoubtedly contributed to the belief, now unfounded, that wine, to be good, must be imported. During the so-called "dry" years, the vines in California, Ohio, New York, and elsewhere in the United States were largely uprooted or neglected. Since it takes a good five years for a vine to grow and since, during the years of World War II, labor was at a premium if not unavailable, it was not until after 1945 that the wines of this country regained an excellence.

California wines, which represent over three fourths of our wine production, come almost entirely from the San Francisco area; Napa, Sonoma, Livermore, Santa Clara, and Santa Cruz. Many California wines are made from virtually the same grapes that are used in Europe, for grafts from many European vines have been planted in California. And in Europe, to fight a vine pest, vines have been grafted onto imported American roots.

The grapes for New York wines, including the increasingly respected champagne, grow around the Finger Lakes.

Ohio's white wines, still and sparkling, come from Sandusky and Lake Erie islands. Henry Wadsworth Longfellow, you may remember, sang the praise of Ohio's Catawba; named for an Indian tribe of South Carolina where the reddish grapes of the Catawba were first grown.

In the wine racks at the Longchamps restaurants, where I have rebuilt my wine list to include approximately forty-two wines, with a half bottle, wherever available, to match every regular bottle, there are rare premium wines and excellent imported wines. But more and more I find myself adding United States brands.

As to what wine goes with what food the answer is simple: the wine of your choice. However, just as there are preferences for certain vegetables with certain foods so are there preferences for certain wines with certain foods.

The *apéritif* wines, served before dinner in place of cocktails, are usually a sherry or a vermouth.

Sherry, with its provocative nutty flavor, ranges from a pale to a dark amber. The paler it is the drier it is. At Longchamps we serve it a little cooler than room temperature—except when air conditioning is on—or slightly chilled.

The herb-flavored vermouths, the dry French or sweet Italian, we serve chilled or on-the-rocks.

A dry white table wine, complementary to fish, shellfish, and poultry, may be a golden Rhine wine, fairly dry, a fruity-flavored white burgundy of the palest amber, or a *not sweet* sauterne.

White wines, generally at their peak when about a year old, are served chilled.

A dry red Burgundy or a claret are most persuasive to the flavor of game, steaks, chops, roasts, birds with dark meat, casseroles, or *pasta*.

Tradition has it that red wine, also at its best at about one year of age, should be served at room temperature. This theory originated when rooms, lacking central heating, were decidedly on the cool side. Wine served at the temperature of our modern and frequently overheated rooms is less palatable than when it is brought directly from a cool cellar or refrigerated briefly.

A pink wine, rosé, is excellent with any food, especially with ham. Rosé, always served well chilled, is generally at its best when it is about six months old; after this there's a chance it may turn a little brown. Taste a little brown too!

The most popular sparkling wines, champagne and sparkling Burgundy, need several years' maturation and are sometimes better when they have lain even longer. They should be very well chilled indeed.

A dry champagne, whether it be straw-colored or pink, is the most versatile of all wines. It may be served as an *apéritif* and with every dinner course, including dessert; not, however, with soup. Soup, likely to contain at least a dollop of sherry, is always accompanied by sherry.

A sweet champagne, of course, is served with dessert only.

Other dessert wines are a sweet sauterne, a red or white port, Tokay, and muscatel; all of them sweet and slightly heavy of body.

Now for the bosh about a different glass being needed for every wine; long-stemmed for this, short-stemmed for that, a large bowl for this, a medium bowl for that, and a small bowl for some other thing.

A stemmed and tulip-shaped glass is the only glass required for the service of table wine. This glass, slightly narrower at the top so that it holds the wine's bouquet, is, preferably, perfectly plain. It needs no adornment but the wine.

A wineglass should hold from seven to eight ounces so that when it is half or two thirds filled—to allow the wine room to "breathe"—it will offer four ounces.

Champagne, too, may be served in this all-purpose glass. But there can be no denying it has greater visual appeal in the saucer-shaped, hollow-stemmed goblet designed for it. Also, a roughness at the bottom of the champagne glass's stem activates the wine in the stem so that it bubbles for a long time. Amusingly enough, not long ago, hollow-stemmed champagne glasses were largely ostracized. The wine snobs damned them as vulgar.

Now for the foolishness about smoking being tabu with wine. This, unquestionably, came about because smoking is frowned upon at the gourmet dinners at which guests taste different wines with each course. Obviously, since smoking dulls the palate, it would be as ill-advised for wine tasters as it would be for tea, coffee, or any other kind of tasters.

There's no doubt in my mind that these and other absurdities have held back the appreciation of wine in this country; all the hullabaloo suggesting it to be more trouble than anything could be worth.

There are, too, I regret to say, certain restaurateurs, maître d's, captains, and *sommeliers* who discourage wine drinking. They price wine at from four to eight times its wholesale price. They take advantage of patrons' lack of knowledge to foist the most expensive wines on their cards upon them. And, in even more deplorable instances, they substitute an inferior wine for that which was ordered, bringing forth the lesser bottle, carefully wrapped in a napkin, with bravura and flourishes.

Some *sommeliers* do not merit the chain, key, and tasting cup they wear. These insignia, in a restaurant, hotel, or great house, designate those in charge of the wine. It presupposes not only that a man is knowledgeable about wine but that he has appreciation for that wine which will, most happily, complement the food with which it is served.

There are no shenanigans about wine at Longchamps. Every bottle is priced at exactly twice its wholesale cost, enough to cover its storage and service and leave us a fair profit.

If there is anything about which there is more nonsense

than there is about food, it, unquestionably, is wine. I find this a pity. For it is no more necessary to be an expert to enjoy wine than it is to understand the feeding, butchering, and hanging of beef to enjoy steak. With wine, as with food, it is necessary only to know what we like.

Which brings me, at the close of this chapter, to an old story about an Italian bishop. This bishop, a most discriminating man, assigned his secretary to precede him on a journey and to note those inns at which good wine was available by marking their doors with EST—Latin for "it exists." The secretary had such enthusiasm for the wine served at an inn at Montefiascone that he marked its door three times, EST, EST, EST! Here, so one version of this story goes, the bishop tarried until he died. Which makes it clear enough why the wine of Montefiascone is known as "Est, est, est."

A votre santé.

INDEX

248 INDEX